Lost in the Supermarket

An Indie Rock Cookbook

LOST IN THE SUPERMARKET

AN INDIE ROCK COOKBOOK

By Kay Bozich Owens & Lynn Owens

Soft Skull Press

Library of Congress Cataloging-in-Publication Data

Owens, Kay Bozich.
  Lost in the supermarket : an Indie rock cookbook / Kay Bozich Owens, Lynn Owens.
    p. cm.
  ISBN–13: 978–1–59376–203–2
  ISBN–10: 1–59376–203–8
  1. Cookery. 2. Musical groups—United States. I. Owens, Lynn. II. Title.
  TX714.O947 2007
  641.5—dc22
                              2007032811

Book design and illustrations by Sharon McGill
Printed in the United States of America

Soft Skull Press
New York, NY

www.softskull.com

This book is dedicated to

Jacques Pepin and
Buzz Osborne

Contents

A DATE/TIME
NOISE REDUCTION ☐

A DATE/TIME
NOISE REDUCTION ☐

Opening Track

Music and food. What would we do without them? While it is hard to be certain, we can hazard a guess that there would probably be a lot less dancing, not to mention a bit more starving. Obviously, both are two key elements to a full and complete life. Whatever power their solo projects hold, however, music and food tap a similar vein as a certain peanut butter cup: They are two great tastes that taste great together. More importantly, music and food are significant defining qualities. Just ask any sociologist or anthropologist about how to define a group culture, and you will quickly hear of the importance of food and music. What is true of national cultures is equally true of subcultures and countercultures. Obviously music differentiates the punks from the shoe gazers from the college rockers. Food creates its own groups, with one clear line of demarcation the number of dead animals one is willing to tolerate in the production on the way to one's food consumption. Interestingly, these food and music groups are rarely self contained, overlapping and crisscrossing in fascinating, and sometimes, surprising ways.

Music and food do more than define groups; they also define selves. The old standby, "You are what you eat," has been updated by the youth culture mantra, "You are who you listen to." But it is as much about becoming who you want to be as it is about being who you are. For both of us, punk rock lured us out of the narrow confines of the larger mainstream culture. What many dismiss as nostalgia depends on the close relationship between moving away from childhood and the soundtrack that accompanied it. If music marks the first coming of age, it is food and cooking that often marks the next major milestone: living on one's own. Traditionally, this has been the moment in which people get pulled back into the mainstream and settle down into domestic bliss. But as food becomes increasingly corporate and commodified, cooking for oneself offers a viable way to continue one's life in the underground.

Moments, whether momentous or quotidian, are marked by how they combine music and food. The pair of the two at special occasions is the stuff of clichés: the happy birthday song and birthday cake or the romantic meal with quiet music in the background. These are the clichés that corporate chain restaurants play with such skill, piping the right music into the dining room to give their food the sense of authenticity. More important still, it is often music and food that help us to define, and to create, the pleasures and joys of everyday life. Combining two passions, and doing so in new and creative ways, can more than double the pleasure of either one.

Celebrity chef Anthony Bourdain argues there is a distinct "link of sin" between music (especially "rock and roll") and food: both are about making people happy, involve sensual pleasures, and, uh, well, are tied to people's yearnings to get laid at the end of the night. He maintains that in the English-speaking world, there's always been an uptight contingent that viewed both the gourmands and the rockers as an evil and threatening presence in society. So, are music and food forbidden pleasures? Perhaps...nobody likes gluttony (I think I recall something about it being a sin), and rock/indie rock/punk rock/whatever you call it, is generally considered something the youth partake in, and an unnecessary pleasure one must give up in adulthood. But that's a lie. It is entirely possible to make your food, your music, your life your own, and be happier and more satisfied because of it. A noble goal, but to get there we must not only have a destination, you need a vehicle. Neither gravy train nor chuck wagon, our vehicle for this trip is the rock star. Climb aboard; let's get this show on the road.

Why rock stars? Well, one reason is obvious: We love celebrities almost as much as we love to eat, and, if the media are to believed, some may love celebrities even more than eating (and not just on the pages of *People* and *In Touch* – take a look at any alternative fanzine/website, the underground scene loves it some rock stars, too). Like it or not, it is hard to shake the way it takes famous performers to make abstract principles concrete. Everyone wants to eat like rock stars. Our first run-in with the gastronomical habits of a favorite musician still lives on in our collective memory.

(Cue wavy lines to indicate a distant reminiscence.)

Back in the early 1990s, fed up with the inanities of jumping through college hoops, we dropped out, looking to start something new. Of course, we did what any disaffected punk rock girl and boy living in nowheresville would do – we took off for the big city. Landing in San Francisco, Kay spent her days peddling overpriced vintage clothes to the tourist masses, and spent her (meager) money at night seeing as many bands as she could. Meanwhile, Lynn toiled away making pizzas at a job that a friend, and future founding member of Deerhoof, Rob Fisk got for him. Maybe not the best career trajectory, but we were young and in love with the music (and, as it turned out, with each other). Given that the city was bursting at the seams with so many big wheels in the underground, it was not uncommon to see your favorite bands (the Melvins!) and musicians out on the town. One night after work, while dining at a cheap, yet trendy, diner, who should take a seat at the table right next to us but Genesis P-Orridge and his friends. What? Genesis P-Orridge eating next to us? Longtime Throbbing Gristle fans (by the way, is that edible?), we were at first star struck, and tried to keep our cool (or perhaps create some for ourselves) by keeping quiet, eavesdropping, and casting a furtive glance whenever we thought no one was looking. Soon enough, however, the big question came up: What was he eating? Our luck, unfortunately, had run out. By the time we could steal a good look, we were too late: His empty plate left few clues. But rather than squelching our speculation, it only fueled it. Was he dining on the raw flesh of babies, or perhaps indulging in a more sensible vegetarian fare? Soon enough this escalated into a private game – whenever we would see a new band or buy a new album, all discussions on the quality of the music would inevitably bring ruminations on the eating habits of the band. "They play like vegetarians!" "This sounds like airplane food!"

The backstage pass is one of the most coveted talismans in all of rockdom. Finally, a chance to cut through the façade and meet (and get to really know) the band. But eating habits backstage are rarely under direct control of the bands, particularly those outside the arena rock mainstream. While Van Halen could afford to demand their brown M&M's cleansed from their candy bowl, most indie bands are lucky to have the oddly shaped meat and bread sandwiches suffered by Spinal Tap – that is, if they get any food at all. No, this tour will have to go beyond the backstage all the way off stage. Consider this book a sort of all-access pass to the kitchens of your favorite (and future favorite) bands. Everyone eats, but it's rare that anyone other than food anthropologists investigate who eats what, and why. This book may not fully answer the why, but it certainly can deliver the what. Opening the refrigerator is akin to the irresistible act of opening the medicine cabinet when visiting a friend's house – how does this person really live, and what is their life really like (and do they have any secrets)? And when you open the refrigerators and cupboards of these bands, don't expect to find a MTV Cribs style fridge, barren save for the fifty bottles of nicely chilled Cristal. Lacking the money, not to mention the inclination, to live off a diet of champagne wishes and caviar dreams, these musicians offer something more realistic and more interesting when the dinner bell rings.

Rest assured, this is not about mindless celebrity worship. One of the initial draws of this project (and one that only deepened as it progressed) was the hope that creativity was not limited to music, that the imagination and inspiration of the stage and studio would translate into the kitchen. At first blush, indie music and a recipe book might seem like an unlikely combination. Years ago, cooking (at least in the U.S.) was not regarded as an artistic expression or a proactive, resourceful way of being less reliant on corporate branding or overpriced restaurants, but rather as something inherently suburban and domesticated (i.e., boring and old ladylike). Today, however, we are in the midst of a virtual cooking revolution, in which cooking is considered a worthwhile, fun way of expressing yourself and taking care of your body (and maybe your mind, not to mention your soul).

Cooking for yourself simply extends the DIY ethic of the alternative and indie world. No need to rely on others to produce your daily supper: Do it yourself. Skip the salad bar at the grocery, stay away from the prepackaged dinners to go, and resist the ease of a frozen meal for one. You don't let corporate radio or music moguls dictate what's on your stereo, you take more control of your musical choices. The band that's playing at a small venue in downtown or at the campus club is generally far superior to the high priced concert going on in your city's major arenas. Why? Well, lots of reasons, but one factor is artistic control. Indie bands control their music (not major labels), without as much regard to corporate budgets, album sales, etc. They have allowed themselves the freedom to make the music the way they want to, feeling less dependent on corporations and the executives who run them. So, in this way, they are bucking the system and having more power and choice in their lives. Why do things the ordinary way, the expected way? Stay away from The Black Eyed Peas, and make your own damn black eyed peas. Skip the take-out and take a chance with cooking the same thing at home. Rock and cook with flare and conviction, and put some effort into it. Do it your way, creatively...on stage, in the studio, or in the kitchen.

Although this cookbook features indie label/alternative/punk bands (and often people assume that indie or punk types are exclusively vegetarian), it is not strictly vegetarian, strictly healthy, strictly anything. It is a compilation and study of what people in bands like to eat – be it meat, be it a wonderful soup with complex flavors, or simply a block of tofu. (Overwhelmingly, though, the food is very healthy, tasty, and easy to make – so it might inspire you to either continue eating healthy, or to join the ranks, give up those fat laden fries, and start thinking more seriously about the food you put into your body, and to remember that cooking can be quite the art form in itself.) Still, indie bands often cook healthy, and health conscious people often have the best recipes because their creations are born out of necessity since healthy food is often not abundant in grocery stores and restaurants. Simply put, the healthy options are not always the obvious ones, so these recipes represent a lot of time and creativity figuring out what tastes good and is good for you. Not all of the recipes are low-cal, cruelty-free concoctions, though. While some are happy to show off the cutting edge of their kitchen knife, others prefer to draw on and deepen tradition. Many share family favorites that are made again and again, and originated in a time less neurotic about the relationship between food and health. And these are fun, too, because it's good to splurge once in awhile, and perhaps more importantly, they give you a little insight into the upbringing and influences of your favorite bands. It's a relatively easy process to find out what a band's musical influences are, but it's quite a different story with regard to what's on their dinner table (or tour bus) every night. And tradition need not mean tired and out of touch. Indeed, as any skilled cook or musician will tell you, the real key to a successful composition is effectively blending innovation and custom.

About this Book

Kay has always considered food to be a special and important part of life. She dreamed of the Sunday roast beef dinners she had read about or seen on the many sitcoms she watched growing up in the 70s (somehow that glass of milk every sitcom kid had to accompany his/her dinner always looked better on TV), and occasionally she'd convince her mother to make one. But mostly, her family mundanely ate Mrs. Paul's Fish Sticks, which looked good on the plate, but sat more uneasily on the palate, and in lieu of playing with Barbies, she played with her McDonald's Playskool Playset (eating at McDonald's more accurately depicted her environment than aspiring to be Barbie and date Ken). She embraced food as a significant part of what makes life special and meaningful. Her family's relationship with food was always one of ease, and necessity, and never one of artistic delight and importance, which never really sat well with Kay. If you've got to eat anyway, you might as well learn about the cooking process and be civilized and somewhat sophisticated about it.

Although not vegan, or even vegetarian, there's a part of Kay that finds a commonality with Isa Chandra Moskowitz, author of *Vegan with a Vengeance* and co-host of NYC's *Post-Punk Kitchen*. She's older, has a punk past, and must work in a cubicle to "survive" as an adult. And like her, Kay's grown depressed with the lack of cool cooking icons and resources that are out there. Getting into cooking doesn't mean you are aspiring to be a suburban Betty Crocker. You have to eat every day of your life, so cooking is a skill everyone should cultivate, and you'd be smart to get as many reference points and tips as you can.

Kay's been scouring cookbooks and watching cooking shows on PBS for longer than she'd care to admit. In her constant craving for recipes and new ideas about food, she yearned to know what others ate, and what they liked, and what was on their dinner table at night, or in their van while touring. For both of us, recipes are little jewels or treasures of scientific experiments. We love the surprise ingredient (ooh! Craisins!) that transforms the mundane into something more artistic and triumphant, if not enviable. We appreciate the effort, commitment, and creativity it takes to transform a basket full of products at your local A&P into a desirable and tasty antidote to one's hunger, and something you'd share with your friends, or add to your weekly meal rotation. And this is how we view recipes and food: ways to both decipher people, and learn from them. So, naturally, we wanted to know what everyone else was doing in their kitchens.

The book itself has rather humble beginnings. We just started writing bands to ask them for their favorite recipes. No grand plans, no book contracts, no idea of how it would work out. We just thought we would give it a go and took the plunge. This book is a testament to the fact that unlikely projects can come to fruition, so it never hurts to try. Did we know any of the bands personally? No. Do we have some kind of insider connection? Absolutely not. Most band recipes were obtained via an email request. The fact that bands took the trouble to write a recipe, take a photo or do a drawing, and correspond during their busy touring schedule and personal shit amazed us…and it renewed our faith in "the punk rock." Bands told us about other bands, and told other bands about the book. Blixa Bargeld, of Einstürzende Neubauten, emailed Kay! Sure, it was to decline participating, but still, it was pretty cool. People doing it for themselves, but also for others…a very nice and important subculture within this capitalist and often self-serving world. And some bands did quite a bit for us, such as putting us on the guest list, passing along the information to their friends in other bands who later got in touch with us, or giving us personal email addresses of other friends in bands. Interestingly, we've noticed that it's a small (indie rock) world, after all. Much of the recruitment for the book took place through musician networks. Members of Black Dice room with Animal Collective. Country Teasers members suggested we contact 16 Bitch Pile Up and the A Frames, Seripop (label of AIDS Wolf) introduced us to members of Sunset Rubdown.

This project was all about the chase, of getting the band at the right time, and them having the slightest interest in cooking. It involved lots of reminding, or, um…nagging. More often than not, the bands were not just procrastinating: They were busy. Touring, recording, curating art shows, their own writing, and side projects competed for time. All of these artistic side projects proved a bit troublesome for us initially, but ended up being somewhat inspirational, offering numerous examples of a creativity overload, extending from music talents into other fields. There's certainly no room for complacency in the indie music world. Of course, not everything worked out the way we hoped. There were a lot of unreturned emails and unfulfilled promises of recipes coming "soon." Jello Biafra neither has email nor does he cook, which made him difficult game to hunt. Daniel Johnston doesn't have email either, but his brother was nice enough to contribute for him. Other failed attempts to get recipes were more tragic, such as Nikki Sudden's unsent recipe. He confessed he was not much of a cook, but was willing to submit what he did prepare for himself. Eerily, and sadly, Kay read his obituary about three weeks later.

This book is a tribute to food, and to the bands themselves. Without their generosity, it would have never happened. This book, of course, is no scholarly endeavor, so there's no formal hypothesis needed, but the whole premise was assuming that people in bands do cook, and that was thankfully confirmed in this project. Of course, not all are gourmets, but everyone has their own favorite recollections of food. This book will give you a little more knowledge about the prominent bands in the indie scene today, as well as some more (or a start to your repertoire of) tasty food you can make for yourself and others for every night of the week. Wouldn't you love to make the Animal Collective's Geologist's Shrimp before seeing them live? Now you can.

Use the recipes in this book to eat out less. Save your money for CDs, shows, books, a trip, whatever…but save your money. We are often the first to fall prey to restaurateurs – "I worked all day. I want to be served. I want ambience! I want delicious food!" Well, too often restaurants lack ambience, or whatever ambience exists is disrupted by a screaming child seated RIGHT NEXT TO YOU! Not exactly the relaxing, indulgent experience you craved, eh? And what about when the server forgets about you? You are reduced to a hostage-like state – you need more water, more wine, or the dessert menu, but it's not exactly acceptable to walk into the bar or kitchen to serve yourself.

So stay at home and cook, where you can serve and indulge yourself! It can be more relaxing than you imagine…and more fun when you cook the meals of rock stars. Save your cash, and rock out in your kitchen!

Oh, and one more thing: Most of these recipes are written less formally and more off the cuff than traditional ones. They are written by creative people who like a little experimentation in the kitchen – and also like to keep it simple. They have given you a little bit of rope to play with – try not to hang yourself, but be open to the possibilities for innovation. Let the recipes ease you into cooking, and use your own instincts to alter, add, and omit as you like. This is simply a starting place, not the end. In 1976, the early punk fanzine *Sideburns* published a diagram of three chords, demanding "This is a chord, this is another, this is a third. Now form a band." Consider this book a culinary update to this dictum: "Here is a recipe, here is another, here is a third. Now make some dinner."

Pantry Staples that Will Help Your Dishes Rock

Of course you don't need all of these ingredients, but these are the ones that tend to come up a lot and be most useful if you cook on a fairly regular basis. If you have a small kitchen and not much cash, don't not make a dish because you are without a certain spice – spices are definitely helpful and important in cooking, but don't let lack of funds get in your way. Omit some ingredients if need be. For years, we didn't cook much because recipes with lots of ingredients just seemed out of our price range, but truly we were missing out on valuable cooking lessons and good homemade food. Plus preparing meals at home (no matter how long the ingredient list is) is almost always cheaper than eating out or buying prepared foods at the store. Once you start gathering a repertoire of recipes, you can plan your meals and pantry choices better.

Spices and dried herbs don't spoil, they lose their strength. They should last for approximately one year (some will tell you six months but that's a tad overcautious), if not stored in the sun or by the stove. Smell and taste prior to using to ensure they still retain flavor. If you don't use the spices often enough to justify buying a whole container, try splitting with a friend.

Spices

- **Bay leaves**

- **Cayenne pepper** (an easy way to add heat and easier to digest than black pepper)

- **Chili powder**

- **Chinese five spice powder** (this isn't essential, but it's fun and adds flair to dishes)

- **Cinnamon**

- **Coriander**

- **Cumin**

- **Curry powder**

- **Nutmeg**

- **Oregano** (or just get the Italian Seasoning blend of spices if you seriously need to save money)

- **Paprika**

- **Salt** (brings out the flavor in every dish – kosher salt works well)

- **Spike** (a natural seasoning blend that adds a layer of flavor to almost any food)

- **Tumeric**

Other Foods for the Pantry or Refrigerator

- **Apple cider vinegar**

- **Balsamic vinegar** (Adds a tang to many recipes, including red lentil soup and spinach salads.)

- **Black beans**

- **Brown rice**

- **Canned diced tomatoes**

- **Canola oil**

- **Chickpeas**

- **Concentrated tomato paste – in a tube** (Fun to use and economical too, as you only use what you need and can store the rest.)

- **Couscous**

- **Crunchy peanut butter** (Mix with soy sauce for an impromptu peanut sauce.)

- **Dried pasta**

- **Mayonnaise** (Low-fat if you or your waistline like.)

- **Minced garlic in the jar** (True foodies and chefs will cringe if they see you with this, but it's so much easier than processing fresh garlic.)

- **Mustard** (Dijon, sweet hot, Polish, or another specialty kind that suits your fancy.)

- **Nutritional yeast flakes**

- **Olive oil**

- **Red lentils** (Kay is pleased to have recently developed a taste for these!)

- **Red wine vinegar**

- **Rice wine vinegar**

- **Soba noodles**

- **Soy sauce**

- **Sriracha hot chili sauce – from Thailand** (This is sometimes referred to as Rooster Sauce due to the Rooster likeness on the bottle. Bands seem to love this ingredient!)

- **Tomato paste**

- **Wine for cooking and drinking** (Never buy cooking wine! It's loaded with sodium and is nasty.)

Food Philosophies and the Occasional Tip

Eric Copeland, BLACK DICE

I guess my general relationship with food is rather weird. I get somewhat uptight at times about where my food comes from, maybe not for the right reasons, more out of fear. And I feel best when I eat small amounts all the time, like nuts and fruit and maybe one bigger meal a day. On a rich day I like to have dried mango and tamari almonds. But, when home, I'm trying to learn more about cooking, especially for one. And I've been trying to do one larger recipe on the weekends that I can save throughout the week, like a soup.

Ben Wallers, COUNTRY TEASERS

Porridge tips from a boarding school youth

Porridge fans: 2-½ cups liquid to 1 cup oats. Make one of the cups liquid MILK. Add salt. Get a good heat going under it but PLEASE PUT A TIMER ON OR YOU WILL DEFINITELY BOIL IT OVER AS WE HAVE DONE 70% OF OUR PORRIDGES. You have to get a good heat to create what is called SKIN. We are talking here about the same principle mentioned in Rice Basic reversed. At boarding school, we were served porridge in a Dickensian vat called a Cauldron or Well-metal. When the whole school had been fed, hardcore porridge fans queued up for the SKIN. This was the brown, caramelized, brulee shit at the bottom which had semi-burnt to the pan. It was UNSPEAKABLY TOOTHSOME, ESPECIALLY WHEN SUGARED. It was scraped from the bottom of the pan with a sharp spoon reserved for this purpose. This gold was fought over, and junior boys never got to it unless everyone else was puking on the UNCOOKED LIQUID JELLY BROKEN-SHELLED "BOILED" EGGS THEY SERVED US in the same type of cauldrons. Anyway I'm going on for no reason because I'm grown up now and have learnt that the SKIN lifts itself off the bottom of the pan if you just leave the porridge sitting for a while after you've bruleed it a little and turned the heat off. Then you can stir the SKIN up into the porridge, so that the porridge tastes much nuttier and more caramel than regular porridge.

Eric Odness, CHARIOTS

All I need to live are these three things:

        1 – Hollandaise sauce

        2 – Honey mustard

        3 – Peanut butter

As long as I have these things to spread on my meals, everything is going to be fine.

MISS ALEX WHITE

I basically eat quesadillas 3 times a day...I also eat large amounts of graham crackers.

Even if you aren't in a touring band, it's easy to understand the difficulties of eating on the road – time constraints, money restrictions, and the 7-Eleven. After awhile, poor food choices can have an effect on your body and soul. Still, touring gives you a unique opportunity to explore other locale's food heritage, so take some advice from the pros.

Camilla Wynne, SUNSET RUBDOWN

On tour we end up eating a lot of nasty stuff, mainly the food of truck stops. Touring across the U.S., I've seen things deep-fried that I never would have imagined – worse than Scotland. Items of note include the deep-fried cheese curds served with Ranch dressing, deep-fried cheese ravioli, and deep-fried French toast served with a Dixie cup of melted margarine.

The other major pitfall is the convenience store dinner. Sometimes we can't eat before the end of the night either because there's no time or because of nerves, and sometimes there's no wonderful 24-hour vegan anarchist diner like in Minneapolis, or even a greasy spoon, in which case dinner is offered up at the 7-Eleven. This means Doritos, microwave burritos, and Funyuns. Only wise, well-seasoned tourers who don't drink very much (like our sound engineer, Sharon) have the sense to get something good like yogurt out of the dairy case (though she also sometimes gets questionable "healthy" stuff like shrink-wrapped hard-boiled eggs).

Our saving grace/holy grail was sushi, with Thai a close second. Any chance we could get, that's what we'd eat. It was good, and it cleansed us. Well, that is, until we were betrayed. Spencer and I got half-price sushi in Manhattan one morning before meeting the band to drive to Philly. We ate our lunch in the van. Next thing I knew I was barfing all over the motel balcony. I spent the night on the bathroom floor. At about 4 a.m., I heard Spencer throwing up in the sink. We had to get hopped up on Dramamine for the van ride back to New York, slept through sound check, and had to play the Mercury Lounge with barf buckets on stage. I didn't eat much of anything for the next four days. Mysteriously, our merch man got equally sick a few days later, after a truck stop chicken sandwich. So that was 50% of our touring party down for the count. Very sad, indeed.

This last tour, I brought along a copy of *Roadfood* by Jane and Michael Stern. Unfortunately, we didn't get to use it a whole lot, since a lot of their recommendations are on side roads, and we would often have to just blaze down the interstates, but occasionally we had time to stop. Only one place was bogus, otherwise they led us to rad diners with really quality American food. I think I'll probably bring it along next time. Can't hurt.

Lou Watts, CHUMBAWAMBA

"An army marches on its stomach." (Napoleon Bonaparte)

Food, like sport, art, and the way we wear our trousers, defines our communities. The affluent, powerful West has long since realized that it's cheaper to invade countries with fast food than with tanks. Up go the golden arches, and suddenly some region's defining and unique way with a potato is swamped by homogenous and unhealthy Super-sized, oversalted, cardboardy snacks. To go.

As a band we've had the good luck to travel around the world several hundred times and one thing we feel morally, politically, and for-the-good-of-learning obliged to do is eat the local food. Cold beetroot soup with a hard-boiled egg floating in the middle. Sounds disgusting. It was, but at least we tried it, and it was memorable.

Those strange gray-colored potato parcel things in Poland. Huge bowls of steaming noodles in Japan. The best, wafer-thinnest pizzas in the world in a busy Rome cafe. These foods define places and people. We don't want to live in a world where everything has the same taste, do we? Easy and comfortable and boring. Who makes the best Greek salad? The Greeks, obviously! Yes, we've been bloody lucky to sit at the groaning tables of the world. And luckier still to have learnt to walk the other way when the Big Yellow M says, "Would you like fries with that?"

Eric Copeland, BLACK DICE

We only tend to tour for about six weeks a year, very little compared to a lot. But we've been doing so for about ten years now, so we're becoming familiar with what to expect in each territory. I'd say we eat best on the coasts and major cities in America. Eating healthy has become a bigger priority for all of us in recent years, so often times the middle of the country can be hard. We will eat some shit every once in awhile; our roadie loves Waffle House. But taking care of your diet is one of the few things I try to maintain on tour as so much else is out of your control and can be really hard on your body (sitting all days, heavy load ins, little sleep …). Along with eating well, we also try to try as much local or new food as is presented. For me, this is more the case overseas, where some cuisine is totally new for me. This seems to be a shared way of traveling and eating with lots of travelers (though McDonald's are everywhere). I'd put Portugal, Japan, California, and NYC as food highlights. And I'd say England is my least favorite food place, along with some bleak American heartland stretches.

Mistina, THE PRIDS

Something helpful to those vegans and vegetarians on the road: a copy of John Howley's *Vegetarian Restaurants & Natural Food Stores* guide. www.vegetarian-restaurants.net

Sites to check out:

> www.foodfightgrocery.com
> www.postpunkkitchen.com
> www.veganinblack.com

Food Innovation: Food for Fun and Profit

Food is more than a lifeline; it is even more than a way of life. Food is big business, and it is only growing larger, as food becomes more commodified and commodities become more ediblized. There has been a veritable explosion of new restaurants, and it is not just from the grease fires. Grocery stores, gourmet, ethnic, and plain-Jane, proliferate. Chefs are celebrities and, sometimes, celebrities are chefs. Everyone's clamoring for his/her piece of the pie. And by pie, of course, we mean moolah, wampum, the almighty dollar.

In this chapter, you will find the gastro-entrepreneurial side of some of your favorite bands. Alas, sometimes a life dedicated to pursuing one's singular vision does not always cover the bills, so one has to take on second or third jobs to make ends meet and make sure, at the end of the month, there is food on the table. Of course, sometimes in order to make ends meet, you have to sell the food on the table. But selling food need not require selling your soul. The underground economy of production and consumption is not just a place for music, but for food, too. Sometimes food selling is a prelude to a music career, sometimes they run concurrently, and in one tantalizing example, it is a dream (or, at least, a waffle) waiting to be filled.

Rachel's Favorite Salsa

Trachtenburg Family Slideshow Players

How can we get into this thing you refer to as the Trachtenburg family? So, we've got our families (trust us, uncool) and then you've got a family who: a) is also a band; b) lives in NYC; c) travels around the world touring; and d) just happen to be food entrepreneurs.

Back in the 90s while living in Seattle, Trachtenburg mom Tina sold her very own "Roasted Gourmet Salsa" in twenty local grocery stores. To this day, Tina judges restaurants by how good their salsa is – her philosophy is that if a restaurant has good salsa, everything else will be stellar as well.

Tina

Salsa is one of my favorite and easy things to make. Rachel really loves my salsa for breakfast so I like to always have it available for her. When I was a child my dad made fresh salsa for me. This recipe can vary as far as availability of fresh vegetables.

INGREDIENTS (USE ALL ORGANIC)   *Makes 2 cups*

Use a small saucepan but one big enough for the tomatoes and jalapeños.

2 jalapeños
4 tomatoes
3 cloves garlic
2 teaspoons sea salt
½ cup water
Pinch of cilantro leaves

PREPARATION

1. First boil the jalapeños for 20 minutes.
2. Add tomatoes to pot with jalapeños and boil for another 20 minutes.
3. The salsa is best when you allow the vegetables to cool for 2 to 3 hours in the refrigerator. Blend garlic and salt and ½ cup water.
4. Add jalapeños and tomatoes and blend cilantro into the dish.

Camilla Wynne, SUNSET RUBDOWN

Take note foodies, record collectors, and entrepreneurs – and make sure you scour your neighborhood's porches for underground food stands and record shops. This one happens to be in Montreal.

I am knee-deep in strawberries, making jam for an illegit bakery/record shop on my friend's back porch. Backroom records and Bake-shoppe – should be swell.

Wah-Full 'o' Whatever

Brian

We had this idea for a restaurant. It's called "Wah-Full 'o' Whatever."
We'd sell waffles with all of the square holes in the waffles filled with
whatever you want. This is never going to happen, so we're going to
give away our secrets here.

INGREDIENTS   *Makes 4 to 6 servings*

First you need to make waffles (or just get frozen waffles). Get these things:

1 cup flour
1 tablespoon baking powder
2 tablespoons sugar
1 cup milk (or soy milk)
1 tablespoon oil or margarine

PREPARATION

1. Heat the waffle iron.
2. Sift the dry ingredients into a medium-sized bowl.
3. Add oil and milk to the dry ingredients.
4. Beat until there are no lumps in the batter.
5. Put a full ½ cup of batter in your waffle iron.
6. When the steam starts coming out sides of iron that means they are ready.
7. And then fill the squares with whatever. Here are our top seven ideas:
   - **Wah-Full 'o' Pizza** – cheese and tomato sauce
   - **Wah-Full 'o' Spaghetti** – spaghetti with sauce in holes
   - **Wah-Full 'o' Veggie Burger** – veggie burger between two waffles with a slice of cheese
   - **Wah-Full 'o' Pancake** – blueberries and maple syrup in the holes with a pancake on top
   - **Wah-Full 'o' Ice Cream** – strawberry ice cream in the holes with strawberry syrup on top
   - **Wah-Full 'o' Peas (or Corn)** – peas in holes (or corn)
   - **Wah-Full 'o' PBJ** – peanut butter and jelly in the holes

The Opening Acts:
Dips, Hors d'Oeuvres, and Drinks

Everyone wants to see the headliners, but the opening acts deserve their due. They whet your appetite for the show to come, putting you in just the right state of mind to enjoy the experience. A great opening act neither over-shadows nor undermines the headliner, but complements the sound and feel, without being redundant. Of course, a lame opening band can ruin an entire evening, no matter how good those that follow are. The same is true for food. You don't just want to dive in to the main course – you have to work your way up to it. Appetizers are the key to any successful meal. Hell, if they're good enough, you won't even need a main course. But if they are lousy, you haven't whetted any appetites – you simply wiped them out.

Even if you hope to catch the opening bands, that doesn't mean you need to get to the show too early. The club owners will have you sitting around waiting for the music to start, swilling their overpriced, watered-down hooch. No thanks. Best to stay home for a while, eat a little, drink a little, and then go out and be merry. Here are some ideas to get the evening started right.

Mr. Both's Homemade Tomato Juice
(alcohol optional)   The Spinto Band

The Spinto Band, originally called Free Beer, offers a slightly more complex drink here. And we would recommend including the alcohol, and serving for brunch alongside English muffins with eggs and a Mornay sauce (béchamel sauce with grated Swiss cheese).

INGREDIENTS   *Makes approximately 12 quarts*

½ bushel basket of big ripe tomatoes
3 tablespoons onion salt
4 tablespoons sugar
3 tablespoons celery salt
1 tablespoon parsley flakes
1 teaspoon ground pepper
1 teaspoon oregano
1 teaspoon ground basil
½ teaspoon summer savory
Lemon juice
Worcestershire sauce
Tabasco sauce
Ground pepper
Vodka
1 celery stalk

PREPARATION

1. Get some tomatoes. Allow the tomatoes to ripen for a few days or until they are not so dang firm.
2. Cut out the stem of the tomato and send it through a food mill. This separates the skin and seeds from the meat and juice. If you are feeling ambitious, you can purchase a tomato press of some kind which makes the whole process a bit easier, but that is not how the Quakers did it in 1879. Save the meat and juice in a large pot.
3. Add the spices and bring the mixture to a low boil for 20 minutes, perhaps longer if at a high altitude.

4. Skim off the residue that will rise to the top during the boiling process, fling residue.
5. Meanwhile, bring 12 quart jars and lids to a boil. This step is necessary so you can seal and preserve your juice.
6. After the juice has boiled for 20 minutes, pour it into the hot jars and seal with the hot lids. As the jars cool, they will seal.
7. Then, open a jar. Pour it into a glass, add a bit of lemon juice, Worcestershire sauce, Tabasco sauce and ground pepper. Then put in some vodka, then a celery stalk. Then drink it poolside while gossiping about ex-husbands or ex-wives.

Note: For added pizzazz, mix the juice with equal parts ginger beer when adding the lemon juice, Worcestershire sauce, Tabasco sauce, and ground pepper. Heavenly!

Bloody Diablo

Matt

My food recipes have always been very lackluster, but when it comes to beverages I put some effort into it. One of my favorites that is always evolving, but nearing absolute perfection is my Bloody Mary, or "Bloody Diablo" if you will.

Ingredients

Makes 1 pint

Rim-lining materials:
  lime, black pepper, celery salt,
  chili powder, cayenne pepper
  powder
Ice
5 dashes of red Tabasco sauce
Pinch of crushed red pepper flakes
3 dashes of Worcestershire sauce
2 dashes of red jalapeño sauce

1 to 2 teaspoons Sriracha
  (cock sauce, but not the
  garlic version)
1 teaspoon olive juice
3 to 4 ounces of Vodka
Tomato juice
1 olive
1 kosher dill spear
1 peppericino
1 beer

Preparation

1. Start with a pint-sized glass and use a lime to rim it with a combination of black pepper, celery salt, chili powder, and cayenne pepper powder.
2. Next fill the glass half full with ice (so you have plenty of room for booze) and add red Tabasco sauce, crushed red pepper flakes, Worcestershire sauce, red jalapeño sauce, Sriracha, and olive juice.
3. Now for the vodka: Any vodka will do, but if you really want to feel the flames of Hell I would suggest Absolut Peppar. Either way you go add 3 to 4 ounces, or about a 5-count if you have a speed pour top. Top off the glass with either tomato juice, or my favorite, "Jero's" Jalapeño Bloody Mary Mix.
4. Garnish with an olive, kosher dill spear, and a peppericino. And make sure you have a beer chaser.

Ian's Sun-Dried Tomato Hummus

Japanther

Japanther are a creative, bike loving, absurdly tight punk band who apparently get a lot of their creative energy from their healthy recipes. Ride your bike, motherfucker!

INGREDIENTS

Serves 6 to 8 as a first course

2 cans cheap chickpeas (include ¾ of the water from one can)
Enough tahini to cover the blades of the blender
3 to 4 whole cloves garlic
Lemon juice
Ground cumin seed (a generous palmful)
Sun-dried tomatoes

PREPARATION

Blend well and serve with pitas that you burn over the open flame of the stove.

Greg Ashley's Texas Style Queso

Greg Ashley founded the band The Gris Gris in Oakland, California after moving from his home in Houston, Texas. But leaving the state has only confirmed his connection to it. Now, everything he touches seems to carry the Texas style trademark. Whether it's their Texas style 1960s infused (but definitely not confused) psychedelic sound or their Texas style queso, one thing is certain. Don't mess with Texas style.

Greg

This sounds kind of white trash but I assure that is exactly how all the Mexican joints in Houston make their queso.

INGREDIENTS

Serves 8 to 10 as an appetizer

Half block Velveeta
Whole can Rotel tomatoes
1 tablespoon butter

PREPARATION

1. Melt all ingredients together in a pot over medium heat until all ingredients are warm and blended together.
2. Serve with chips.

Guacamole

Bliss Blood currently lives in NYC and performs Hawaiian swing and 1920s style jazz music as part of The Moonlighters, among other bands. Back in the day, she was the lead singer of Pain Teens, a staple on the Trance Syndicate label. Bliss occasionally sings on other bands' recordings, most notably Swans and Melvins.

Bliss claims she's not really much of a cook, but she does have a few simple things she makes a lot, this recipe being one of them. Other frequent dishes on her dining table include hummus and veggies.

This guacamole is perfect for parties – it's fat content makes it seem a little decadent, but it's still relatively healthy. Watch it go fast. For additional festivity, try serving in a Mexican mortar and pestle, or Molcajete y Tejolete, which is made from volcanic rock. They are available online for under $20.

INGREDIENTS   *Makes approximately 1 cup*

1 large jalapeño, seeds and ribs removed
1 small onion or ½ cup chopped white part of leek
1 handful of sun-dried tomatoes
Juice of one lemon
Salt and pepper, to taste
2 avocados

PREPARATION

1. Combine all ingredients except avocado in food processor.
2. After ingredients are blended, add avocado and blend until almost smooth.

Gorch Fock Stickers

Like a force that refuses to be reckoned with, Gorch Fock are an explosive, heavy band featuring dual drummers who face off during performances. Surprisingly, these sludge masters are also foodies who fancied having a cook-off at their record label to decide on a contribution. Well, time didn't permit for the cook-off, but chances are this tasty concoction would have been a contender.

Joey

While in Beijing, on an extended shore leave from the port of Shanghai, we picked up a traditional Gyoza recipe. After combining it with tastes from several other ports, we have come up with this favorite appetizer. This recipe makes a batch sized to feed any large group, and is easy to toy around with. This treat is a great vehicle for all kinds of sauces from Siracha to ranch dressing. I have not included any information about how to make the dough, however it is not incredibly difficult if you do a little research. If you find yourself unable to eat meat, from too many long trips at sea, you will find that most commercially available wrappers are just frozen flour, water, and salt.

The traditional recipe often involves pork, and can be added if you like. Enjoy this favorite knowing that if you can't get them, you can always make Gorch Fock Stickers for all of your friends.

INGREDIENTS   *Serves 4 to 6*

2 tablespoons garlic, chopped
1 lobe ginger, grated
1 cup parsley, chopped
1 teaspoon extra virgin olive oil
2 cups button mushrooms, chopped
1 cup shitake mushrooms, chopped
2 cups bok choy, chopped
1 packet chopped organic tempeh (8 ounces)

1 cup vegetable stock
6 ounces dried miso (or fresh equivalent)
1 cup nori, chopped
1 dried onion, chopped
1 teaspoon rice vinegar
1 teaspoon sesame oil
1 teaspoon cornstarch or starch equivalent
1 tablespoon soy sauce
Frozen Gyoza wrappers (or fresh equivalent if you know how)

PREPARATION

1. In a medium saucepan sweat the ginger, garlic, and parsley in olive oil over a medium-high heat. Add the button mushrooms and cook, stirring often, until most of the moisture is gone.
2. Add the shitake mushrooms and the bok choy and cook again until most of the moisture is gone. Add the tempeh and reduce the heat to medium and cook 5 minutes.
3. In a separate container combine the stock, miso, nori, onion, rice vinegar, sesame oil, and starch to make a sauce.
4. Add the sauce to the pan and increase the heat.
5. Stir and cook until the sauce thickens completely.
6. Remove from the heat and let rest 15 minutes.
7. On a lightly floured board roll 1 tablespoon of the filling in a wrapper folding the ends together and pinching the top. The goal is to make each dumpling look like a little Gorch Fock sailing ship. Fry the dumplings in a large sauté pan or wok coated in oil, on a high heat, until the bottoms turn brown.
8. Add 2 cups of water and cover. Steam the dumplings for 10 to 15 minutes.

James' Tomatoless Salsa

Sorry About Dresden

Let's play six degrees of Sorry About Dresden. They live in Chapel Hill, North Carolina, where Lynn went to grad school. They seem to be sorry, which is Kay's natural state (she's ever so sorry). They are the second band in this book to reference Dresden, Germany. Guitarist Matt is the brother of Saddle Creek Records' owner Justin Oberst, and Bright Eyes' singer Conor. Is that six yet?

Regardless, the forces of the universe seemed to be aligning to bring them into our book. Alas, connections might get you through the front door, but it's content that allows you to stay. That is, when all is said and done, we don't care who you know or where you're from. If the music ain't tasty and the recipe don't rock, then we're not interested. Luckily for all of us, that's not the case here. Salsa is the number one condiment in the world these days, and with this recipe you just might be getting the number one compliment for your number one condiment. Try it. You won't be sorry (even Kay wasn't!).

This recipe is 100% vegan.

The amount of each ingredient you add to this is entirely up to you. Red, yellow, and orange bell peppers can be used interchangeably for color and flavor.

INGREDIENTS

Makes 2 to 3 cups

1 small red onion
Bunch of green onions
1 red bell pepper
1 yellow bell pepper
Bunch of radishes
1 to 2 jalapeño peppers
2 habañero peppers
Handful of cilantro, chopped
Sea salt, to taste
Juice of 1 to 3 limes (depending on how juicy you want it)
1 avocado, ripe yet firm

1. Dice the onions and bell peppers.
2. Chop up the green onions, all of the white part and as much of the green part as you can.
3. Cut the radishes into matchsticks (if you have a slicer that can julienne, use it).
4. Mince the hot peppers as finely as you can. And for the love of god, wear gloves. It's not less manly.
5. For the best way to get an avocado out of its shell, see below. Add the avocado, cilantro, sea salt, and lime juice.

James

I like to mix lightly salted blue and white corn chips. Don't skimp on the chips, and if I hear about you using those Tostito's Lime-flavored chips, I WILL hunt you down. You didn't do all that fucking work to ruin it with crappy chips.

Okay, the avocado. I've never tried to describe it in print, so forgive me if I'm unclear.

1. First, cut the avocado from top to bottom, cutting around the pit. Twist the two halves and separate into two pieces.
2. Carefully jab the knife into the pit and twist it out.
3. While still in its shell, cut through the meat of the avocado checkerboard style. If you hold the avocado half in your palm and slice gently, you can feel the tip of the knife scratching against the shell. I said *gently*.
4. Then use a spoon to scoop out a little at a time. If the avocado is firm, you'll have nice little chunks. If not, you'll have goo.

Haas avocados are easiest to find, but other varieties might be firmer. Try throwing them in the freezer for 20 minutes before slicing. (Also, if you put your onions in the freezer for a half hour or so before chopping, you'll experience less weeping.)

Red Headed Sluts

Ben

RED HEADED SLUTS as taught to me by the great Abby of Spartanburg, South Carolina, in the great UNCLE DOCTOR'S venue:

INGREDIENTS   *Serves 1*

1 ounce Jägermeister
1 ounce Peach Schnapps
Cranberry juice

Get Potlucky Tonight

Another day, another goddamn potluck. Don't get me wrong, potlucks are beautiful things: They provide wonderful ways for friends to get together, commune with natural grace, and eat a wide variety of food without putting anyone out. But the food often leaves a lot to be desired.

Inevitably, for most people, the night before or the day of the event, this invitation becomes more of a hassle – stuff came up, you don't know what to make, and dammit, why can't you just meet at a restaurant? Too often potlucks produce tables crowded with tired casseroles and bowls upon bowls of chips, leaving us feeling a weird sense of déjà vu of childhood family reunions held in a potato chip factory. Hey, we like you guys, but wasn't this supposed to be about the food? Yeah, we'll eat it, but that doesn't mean that we're going to like it.

Potluck need not be synonymous with bad luck. Don't wait until the last minute and then pick up a six-pack and a bag of pretzels on the way to the party. This will get you in the door, but just barely. And don't think you can get away with just splurging for a bit more (or a bit better) alcohol. There are plenty of ways to raise the bar without raising your bar tab. Beyond these boring concoctions is a world of delicious whimsy and whimsical delicacies. The change needs to start with you. Instead of doing the very least, do just a little bit more and see how much more popular you become. Watch as your friends' eyes light up when you walk in and plonk your Gummi Bear salad on the table! The squeals of delight will be so loud they will easily drown out the foot shuffling of shame from the people who brought the celery with Cheese Wiz. Enjoy the attention, but recognize that those lovely laurels coming your way won't provide you a place to rest. You just started the great potluck arms race; now no one will be satisfied with the same-old same-old. But that's okay, because now everyone will be a winner and potlucks will never again be a "celebration" to fear, but rather a fare to celebrate.

Gummi Salad!

Bassist Bryan Poole used to deliver pizzas to frat boys in between touring and recording, and more importantly, he admitted to wanting to kill them! We wonder how many indie rockers have had to resort to delivering pizzas to pay the rent. We had a friend who got fired from Domino's because his pants weren't shiny enough (translation: they weren't Polyester). Oh the disgrace of working for a living! When you are off work, however, you must make every meal and potluck count, starting with Gummi Salad!

INGREDIENTS/PREPARATION   *Serves a large crowd*

Jimmy

When I moved to Athens, Georgia, many people in town were having potluck dinners at their houses. This is not to say that I had never experienced potluck dinners elsewhere, but it seemed to be happening quite often in Athens around the time I moved here. Although I do cook, I usually found myself pressed for time in these situations…so I invented the GUMMI SALAD.

Basically there's nothing to it. Just go to the store and find as many different shapes of Gummis as you can discover/afford. Then bring the Gummis home. Find a large bowl. Mix all the Gummis together in the bowl. And toss. It's that simple and from my experience it has been a big hit at potlucks.

Since there is not a list of ingredients for this recipe I thought I'd give a list of interesting Gummi styles that I have come across throughout my travels (starting with the classics):

Bear	Life Savers	Mushroom	Wrench
Worm	Hamburger	Boobs	Saw
Fruit	Hot Dog	Penis	Level
Ring	Pizza	Barf	Bottle Opener
Sours	French Fries	Bone	Ferrari
Fish	Teeth	Peace Sign	Snake
Hearts	Tooth	Lips	Etc.
Dolphin	Tennis Racket	Bottle	
	Soccer Player	Hammer	

John's Mexican Lasagna

Pengo are a noisy, genre-defying band from Rochester, New York. Their recipe may seem like a lot of trouble, but it's a great dish to make ahead and then heat up when you need it. A salsa-based sauce with loads of cheese and sour cream – it's the ultimate crowd pleaser.

This Mexican lasagna is a welcome makeover for the more traditional Italian-style lasagna.

While this recipe is easy to make, it is time consuming.

It's best to break it up into three parts.

Part 1: The Chicken

INGREDIENTS   *Serves 8 to 10*

About 10 pounds of chicken. You can usually find quartered chickens at
   your local supermarket or public market.
4 cloves garlic, peeled and minced
2 teaspoons oregano, crumbled
2 teaspoons salt
4 bay leaves
1 teaspoon black pepper

PREPARATION

1. In two wide 5-quart pans evenly distribute the chicken parts. Add cold water to cover by about 1 inch and set over medium heat.
2. Stir in an equal amount of the garlic, oregano, salt, bay leaves and black pepper into the two pans and bring to a simmer. Partially cover the pans and lower the heat.
3. Simmer the chicken, turning it once at the halfway point, until the meat is tender and falling off the bone. This takes about 25 minutes.
4. Remove the pan from the heat, set it on a rack and let the chicken cool to room temperature, uncovered in the liquid. Drain the chicken. Then skin the chicken and remove and shred the meat. Cover and refrigerate.

Part 2: The Sauce

6 long green chilies

3 tablespoons olive oil

3 cups onion, finely chopped

3 cloves garlic, peeled and minced

2 teaspoons ground cumin

1-½ teaspoons oregano

2 cups chicken broth

2 cups tomato-based bottled hot salsa

2 teaspoons salt

PREPARATION

1. Preheat your broiler and roast the long green chilies, turning them until they are evenly charred on each side. Steam the chilies in a bowl covered with a plate until cooled.
2. Rub away the burned peel and then stem and seed the chilies. Chop up the chilies.
3. Warm the olive oil in a 3-quart pan over low heat. Add the onions, garlic, cumin and oregano and cook, covered, stirring once or twice for 15 minutes.
4. Stir in the chicken broth, salsa, green chilies, and salt and raise the heat. Bring the mixture to a boil and then lower the heat slightly. Stir the mixture every couple of minutes and cook uncovered for about 20 minutes.
5. Cool the sauce to room temperature. Take 2 cups of the sauce and set aside for later. Combine the remaining sauce with the shredded chicken.

Part 3: Assembly

INGREDIENTS

....

2 cups corn oil
24 six-inch corn tortillas
2 cups sharp cheddar cheese, shredded
2 cups Monterey jack cheese, shredded
16 ounces sour cream

....

PREPARATION

1. Preheat oven to 350°F.
2. In a deep skillet, heat about 1-inch of corn oil over medium heat.
3. Using tongs, immerse the tortillas one at a time in the oil, then turn them. The tortilla should have slight bubbling on their surface, they shouldn't be in the oil for longer then a few seconds.
4. Transfer the tortillas onto absorbent paper.
5. Arrange 8 of the tortillas in an overlapping layer in the bottom of a 10 x 14-inch backing dish about 2 inches deep.
6. Spread half of the chicken over the tortillas. Arrange 8 more tortillas in an overlapping layer over the chicken. Combine the shredded cheese and sprinkle half of it over the tortilla.
7. Spread the remaining chicken over the cheese. Arrange the 8 remaining tortillas over the chicken. Spread the reserved sauce over these tortillas. Sprinkle the remaining cheese over the sauce.
8. Spread the sour cream over the cheese.
9. Bake about 45 minutes. Let the lasagna stand for about 5 minutes until you try and serve it. I have also found that if you refrigerate the whole dish and reheat it the following day it tastes even better. (Make sure you don't directly put a refrigerated casserole dish into a hot oven – it will likely crack. Let sit until food and dish come to room temperature, and then stick in the oven!)

Note: For a more attractive finish, sprinkle with olives, additional cheese, and green onions before serving.

Rose des Sables (Sand Roses)

Call Me Loretta is a cool band from France, who manage to produce songs that could just as easily serve as soundtracks to your dreams or your nightmares.

Seb

For when you are invited to a reception with the queen, presidential dinner, wedding anniversary, Tupperware party, housewarming party, dinner with your step-mother, a wake, or for any other formal occasion. And you are supposed to bring dessert and buy roses for the lady of the house. Of course, you are too hung over to get to the florist before it closes. Instead of disappointing everyone (again, as usual), or stealing a cooling pie from your grandmother's windowsill (you heartless bastard), you can cook sand roses and kill two birds with one stone.

INGREDIENTS   *Serves 10*

¾ cup butter
8 ounces chocolate chips
5-½ ounces confectioners' sugar
8 ounces cornflakes

PREPARATION

1. In a pot, melt the butter on low heat.
2. Once the butter has melted, pour the chocolate chips in the pot.
3. Use a wooden spoon to add the confectioners' sugar. Stir until the mixture is smooth.
4. Add the cornflakes, stir thoroughly, and remove pot from the stove.
5. Using a coffee spoon, drop mixture into small lumps on a sheet of tinfoil.
6. Let cool on tinfoil. Wait until they have become solid. In the meantime, you can get dressed to the nines. Then, remove from the tinfoil with a knife.
7. The roses are ready to eat!

If you are a worldly man/woman-about-town, present the roses like a bouquet of flowers. First, shape tinfoil into a cone resembling the plastic wrapping of real flowers, then pile your sand roses into the opening on top for that special effect. More delicious than the "real" thing.

Enjoy!

Note 1: You can also cook sand roses for any informal occasion or to satisfy your own gluttonous desires.

Note 2: You can also follow the lead of our drummer, and give these "roses" to ladies/men you're trying to pick up (without overtly appearing to do so).

Note 3: Don't follow the advice of Note 2 in a restaurant.

World Tour

The world tour — the dream of musician and vagabond alike. There's nothing like packing up the passport and taking off to see and experience the world. In our early misspent youths of arena rock fandom, we remember ogling over the overpriced tour merch tables, with a special eye for the tour T-shirt. The tour T-shirt served multiple purposes, the main one being to fill the coffers of the band management. But for the fans, it was about signaling one's presence at the event. In school, we remember, the day after any "big" concert, it was always fun to count all the people who wore their tour shirt the very next day to let everyone know what they were up to the previous night (the "cooler" people would, of course, hold off for a few days, knowing that the appearance of trying so hard is the sure kiss of death to any highly cultivated aura of cool). But the shirt does more than attach the fan to the band, it also links them into the chain of travel, as noted by the required list of dates and exotic cities. Paris: Oooh-la-la! London: Swinging! Berlin: Achtung! The world tour emphasizes the truly global nature of music, highlighting similarities across differences across the world.

But it is not just the 16-tour-bus bands who set out on world tours, just like it is not just the rich and famous who crisscross the globe as travelers. For alternative/indie bands, the tour is the outreach program the big labels handle by slathering their star de jour all over MTV and Rolling Stone. But when your PR budget can't (or won't) cover all the wheel-greasing necessary to get the attention of the "opinion makers," you are left with only one choice: to take your music directly to the fans. Crossing the border only extends this process, offering the opportunity to tap new audiences and sometimes to revel in a celebrity status unknown back at home, as when they are "big in Japan."

But what about me? What am I to do, stuck in this boring job, in this boring town, in this boring country? Even if you can't afford the time and money needed to globe trek, there are plenty of options available to bring the taste of the foreign into your life, emphasis on taste. Foreign and ethnic restaurants are everywhere, even in the middle-of-nowheresville. From the ritzy-glitzy sushi restaurant downtown to the Olive Garden out by the mall, there seems to be something for everyone. Everyone, that is, except for those who want to skip the restaurant, and enjoy their own world tour from the comfort of their home. For those occasions, we offer the following ideas.

Geologist's Greek Style Shrimp
Animal Collective

Full disclosure: Sometimes we like to read the reviews on Amazon.com for our friend's books or other stuff we're interested in. This exercise is less about seeking advice on potential purchases, and more about getting into people's heads. It's a bit voyeurstic, but it's a useful measure to see "what America's thinking." So, one of the Animal Collective reviewers on Amazon.com seemed really perplexed by the band. All of this guy's friends were into them, he'd read many favorable critical reviews, but he just didn't get them. Frustrated, he declared, "…this stuff is really regressed and disturbing. I imagine these guys on acid running around naked in the mud pretending to be five years old while making jungle sounds into a tape recorder." For us, and probably you, there's no higher compliment to give. What's not to get?

When not running around naked in the mud, Brian cooks a lot, usually steamed vegetables, rice, and grilled meat of some kind. The only special dish he claims to make is this Greek Style Shrimp. He doesn't like to measure, but prefers to "eyeball it" – which is the way a lot of people prefer to cook …no measuring spoons, less dishes to wash, and less restrictive!

INGREDIENTS   *Serves 2 to 3*

3 cloves garlic, pressed
1 yellow onion, chopped
2 medium tomatoes, chopped
1 pound **WILD CAUGHT** shrimp (no imported farmed shrimp please!)
Oregano
Black pepper, to taste
1 cup white rice
1 handful of feta cheese, crumbled

PREPARATION

1. Simmer garlic and onions in olive oil until the onions are sweet. Make sure the garlic doesn't burn. Add the tomatoes and simmer on medium-high heat. Stir often until the excess liquid boils off and the tomatoes become pulpy.
2. Add the shrimp and cook until done.
3. Add oregano and pepper to get your desired spice level. When finished, pour over top of cooked white rice.

4. Crumble a bunch of feta cheese over the top and then stir the cheese into the dish. This dish is best when served hot because the cheese melts and is distributed evenly throughout the dish, but it also works well as a cold leftover dish the next day.

Malmo Tomato Soup

The American Analog Set

The American Analog Set have been critical indie darlings for years. Formed in Texas, they've actually been touring Europe frequently the last several years, although it appears that their touring has dried up now due to other obligations. If you find yourself yearning to see the band come to your town, you may have to resign yourself to the fact that it may not happen, and drown your sorrows in this rich and comforting soup, discovered by the band while on tour in Malmo, Sweden.

The American Analog Set

This soup is necessary. This soup doesn't quit. This soup doesn't pretend to be something it's not...because this soup doesn't front. I loaned this soup $5 and the soup was there the next day like...boom ..."Here's that $5."

INGREDIENTS   *Serves 6*

2 yellow onions, chopped
1 tablespoon unsalted butter
3 cloves garlic
* 1 can passata tomatoes
2 cubes Bouillon
2 tablespoons sugar

6 tablespoons fresh coriander, minced
1 can coconut milk
5 Thai peppers, chopped
Cumin, salt, and pepper, to taste

RECOMMENDED ON THE IPOD:

"Obsessed with Excellence" by Les Savy Fav

Note: There are many varieties of canned tomatoes. Passata tomatoes are very popular in the U.K., and are basically skinless, seedless, unflavored, uncooked tomato pulp. If you can't find a can at your grocer, you can drain and sieve regular canned tomatoes (using a food mill helps). Don't substitute tomato paste – it's too sweet and concentrated. Also, don't use tomato sauce! It's thinner and has added seasonings that you don't want in this soup.

1. In a medium saucepan, sauté yellow onions in 1 tablespoon unsalted butter, stirring occasionally for 7 minutes.
2. Add garlic. Add tomatoes and bouillon cubes in water (consult directions on box for appropriate amount). Simmer for 10 minutes.
3. Add sugar, coriander, coconut milk, and thai peppers. Simmer for another 10–15 minutes.
4. Add cumin, salt, and pepper to taste. Serve.

Thai Sweet Potato Soup

Belle and Sebastian

Belle and Sebastian really need no introduction: They are one of the most critically acclaimed bands of our time. And this soup, like the band, seems to please all. It has so many layers of flavor – the end result is a beautifully textured and complex soup. The ingredients used to seem exotic, but you should be able to find them at your local grocery store, or a more upscale one.

INGREDIENTS   *Serves 8*

1 large onion, peeled and chopped
2-inch chunk of fresh ginger or galangal, peeled and chopped finely
1 tablespoon Thai red curry paste
1 stalk lemongrass, chopped
2 cloves garlic, crushed or finely chopped
2 sweet potatoes, peeled and thinly sliced
3-½ cups good vegetable stock (such as Swiss Bouillon)
1-¾ cups coconut milk
Juice of half a lime
* 4 or 5 dried Kaffir lime leaves

* optional

PREPARATION

1. Start by frying the onion with the ginger, curry paste, and lemongrass. Fry until soft.
2. Add the garlic and fry for a further minute.
3. Add the sweet potatoes and the stock.
4. Bring to a boil and simmer for 20 minutes, or until the sweet potato is soft.
5. Add the lime juice, lime leaves (if using), and the coconut milk, and liquidize.
6. If you like it hotter, add a red chili (seeded and chopped) at the start (along with the onion).

Okonomiyaki

Dmonstrations are an obvious choice for an indie rock cookbook since Tawaraya Tetsunori's frenetic lyrics are often focused on food. Okonomiyaki (literal translation "as you like") is a staple of Japanese cuisine, popular for a relaxed and informal quick bite. The name references the versatility of the dish, with many cooks varying the ingredients and additions depending on mood and tastes. Most often compared to a pancake, others say it is more like a Japanese pizza, since it's not sweet and the "toppings" can vary widely. Kay ate Okonomiyaki with some Japanese friends in Tokyo, and enjoyed it quite a bit, until the restaurant started shaking due to a minor earthquake. Her Japanese friends declared her very lucky, to simultaneously experience her first earthquake and Okonomiyaki.

INGREDIENTS   *Serves 2*

8 ounces flour	8 ounces water
2 eggs	1 teaspoon baking soda
Little bit of seaweed juice	Pinch of sugar
8 ounces cabbage, sliced well	Pinch of salt
Pinch or 2 of red ginger	

PREPARATION

1. Mix all ingredients well in a bowl.
2. Form into a flat circular formation.
3. Put in an oiled sauté pan, cook it as if it were a pancake over medium heat. When it starts to brown on one side, it's time to flip the Okonomiyaki.
4. Place the following condiments on the top of your creation:
   - Dried seaweed (it's like a powder)
   - Shredded dried bonito flakes
   - Japanese "Cupie" mayonnaise (Available at Asian markets, you'll know it when you see it – the packaging has a Cupie Doll on it.)
   - "Otafuku sauce" or even bulldog sauce
5. EAT IT!!!

 Note: You can put pork or beef in this dish if you eat meat.

Autumn/Winter Nabemono

Pretty Girls Make Graves

Pretty Girls Make Graves, unfortunately, are now in their final resting place. During the course of starting and finishing this book, their drummer Nick Dewitt, decided to leave the band. The rest of the band felt it best not to continue the band without him. Here's hoping that these talented Seattle musicians keep producing great music from beyond the Pretty Girls Make Graves grave.

In the meantime, Pretty Girls do more than make graves – they also make dinner. This wonderful recipe comes from keyboardist Leona K. Mars.

Leona

Nabemono is a general term for a hot pot dish in Japan. There are many different kinds of nabe but this one is my favorite. This dish is meant to be eaten at the table over many hours and with a lot of sake or beer. I have been to nabe (hot pot) parties that were over six pleasant hours and resulted in everyone simply laying down and falling asleep together. It is my favorite small party dish and one that my family enjoys many times throughout the chilly seasons.

Hot Pot

INGREDIENTS   *Serves 3 to 4*

1 Chinese cabbage, chopped into 1-inch pieces
1 leek, chopped into 1-inch pieces
Any bunch of Asian greens (I like the slightly bitter ones)
1 Daikon radish (¾ sliced for the dish and set aside ¼ grated for sauce)
* Agedashi tofu pouches (½ per person eating)
* Mochi (1 per person eating) – which goes inside the agedashi and seals with a toothpick
* Any fresh white fish (halibut, cod, and snapper work well and are usually easy to find: ½ pound per person)
1 soft tofu, cut however you like

* optional. This makes a great vegetarian dish as well.

Sauce

INGREDIENTS   *(Yields 1 cup which serves roughly 3 people)*

Juice from ½ organic lemon
½ teaspoon lemon rind
½ teaspoon grated ginger
1 part water
1 part soy sauce
2 tablespoons rice vinegar
Dash of red pepper

Note: The amounts of water and soy sauce vary depending on how much lemon juice you get from your lemon.

PREPARATION

1. Have everything chopped and ready to go near the table because you will be adding to the hot pot as you eat it.
2. Start by boiling 8 cups of water on the stove and adding some Chinese cabbage.
3. Throw in some leeks and then take the pot to the middle of the table.
4. Start adding a bit of everything.
5. Once things are boiled and ready to eat, use a slotted spoon and have everyone serve themselves into their bowls which each already contain ¼ cup of the sauce. I usually save the agedashi tofu/mochi pouches for the end but it's up to you.
6. Serve with fresh rice on the side.
7. Enjoy!!!

Plokkfiskur

Mugison is a former sailor whose music outsells Björk and Sigur Rós in his native Iceland. His tours are legendary, and we've always been intrigued with his creation "The Mugibox" – a suitcase-sized box that contains everything Ornelius Mugison needs to go out on the road, including clothes and music equipment. Here's one of Mugison's favorite dishes, a traditional Icelandic fish-stew or Plokkfiskur.

INGREDIENTS   *Serves 6*

1-¼ pounds fresh haddock
10 ounces potatoes
3 tablespoons REAL butter (not one of those "I can't believe it's not butter" types) or margarine
Olive oil (enough to coat the bottom of the pan)
1 onion
Dash of flour
Milk
Black pepper
Salt

PREPARATION:

1. Boil the potatoes and the fish.
2. Fry the onion in the oil and then fry everything together for a short while you melt the butter in a separate saucepan (do not overheat).
3. Throw some flour in the saucepan and stir hard. You should get some kind of a butterdough (or roux).
4. Add dash of milk and keep stirring hard. Continue adding some milk and stir until you get a thick white sauce.
5. Pour contents of saucepan over the fish, potato, and onion.
6. Stir in spice (lots of salt and pepper).
7. Eat with toasted bread or Icelandic rúgbraud, lots of butter on the bread.
8. Drink cold milk or beer with it…nothing else!

Phal Ras

The prolific John Darnielle, songwriter and half of the 4AD band The Mountain Goats, is noted for his beautifully crafted songs, which are often about food and animals that can talk! John borrows the recipe of world-renowned actor and cookbook author Madhur Jaffrey to create a refreshingly pungent drink. Take John's lead and read different cookbooks for ideas you'd never come up with on your own.

Phal Ras (which is to say "Ginger Fruit Punch")

Adapted freely from *Madhur Jaffrey's World Vegetarian* cookbook, 1999 Clarkson Potter publishers.

INGREDIENTS *Makes 1 pitcher*

---

1 8-inch piece of fresh ginger, peeled and coarsely chopped
1 cup sugar
1 cup fresh (I repeat *fresh*) lemon or lime juice
1-½ cups fresh orange pineapple juice
3 cups club soda
Ice cubes
* ½ cup Guava juice for variety if you like

---

* optional

PREPARATION

1. Combine ginger, sugar, and 1 cup of plain water in a heavy pan.
2. Bring to a gentle boil, stirring constantly; any time you're cooking with sugar on a stovetop, you wanna be careful not to over-boil things.
3. As soon as it boils, reduce the heat to low. Simmer, uncovered, stirring occasionally, for fifteen minutes. What you have now is a syrup. You may look at it and say, "I think of syrups as being more viscous than this here, Jethro," and frankly I share your concern, but any sugar/water/flavor infusion used to flavor a drink is a syrup regardless of its viscosity! Live and learn, eh?

4. Strain the syrup into a pitcher and let it cool. Be careful straining – hot sugar will burn you with a quickness. G'head and throw the ginger away, or into the compost collector, though it's real sugary and will attract mad ants.
5. When the delicious gingery syrup has cooled, add the lemon juice and the orange pineapple juice and the club soda.

John Darnielle

Madhur Jaffrey insists that plain water "is just as good" but I wouldn't know, because the club soda is so wonderful and delicious that I do not take any chances messing with the working formula, to wit: ginger-sugar syrup + fresh-by-God lemon juice + orange pineapple juice + plenty of ice + club soda = a drink so fine you'll wonder where it's been all your life. Enjoy!

Yorkshire Pudding

Chumbawamba

Chumbawamba are anarchists who have been playing music for three decades. They are known for their political activism, and a certain song called "Tubthumping," hugely popular in 1998. The band used their significant profits to help political organizations, and are still active in music and political work. They bring a traditional English pudding to the table.

Lou

So here's a dish specially from our little cultural backwater, traditional and popular and homemade. It's something we're proud of, and it keeps our bellies full as we fight hand-to-hand with the invading army of red-wigged clowns. Ladies and gentlemen, we give you: The Yorkshire Pudding.

A traditional dish from Yorkshire customarily served with roast beef and potatoes and vegetables. Works well with veggie sausages and gravy.

INGREDIENTS

Serves 6 as a side dish

2 heaped tablespoons of plain flour
Generous pinch of salt
$^{1}/_{2}$ cup milk
1 egg
Sunflower oil

PREPARATION

1. Mix the above ingredients with a spoon and then a whisk.
2. Add $^{1}/_{2}$ cup milk and continue to whisk for a few minutes.
3. Leave to stand for at least half an hour, preferably for a few hours.
4. Heat the oven until very hot (at least 200°C, which is about 400°F)
5. Put a drop of sunflower oil into Yorkshire pudding tins, these are slightly bigger than bun tins. (You can use one large tin if you don't have smaller ones.) The key to success is getting the oil very hot before adding the mixture – it should be just smoking.

6. Pour in the mixture and cook in a hot oven for about 10 to 15 minutes until the puddings are nicely risen and golden. The larger size puddings will take longer than the smaller ones.
7. Take out and serve immediately.

Cheap Eats, Cheap Thrills

It's the end of the month, bills are piling up, and you're hungry. All that splurging a couple weeks ago seemed like a good idea at the time, but now it's time to settle your accounts. We have had it drilled into our heads that you get what you pay for, and after years of squeaking by on Ramen Noodles, you should just about be convinced of that fact. Cheap food doesn't seem to satisfy many desires, except perhaps the desire not to starve to death. But cheap food hasn't only been sold cheap; it's also been sold short. Just because you don't have much scratch doesn't mean you can't cook up a meal from scratch. You don't have to scrape the bottom of the barrel at dinnertime.

Bands know a thing or two about squeezing the most nutrition and richest flavor out of their last dime. While they wait for the royalties to start rolling in, they found creative, and delicious, answers to life's burning question: "How can we feed everyone with the spare change we found in the couch?"

The Country Teasers! Kay loves B. R. (or Ben or The Rebel) Wallers' grad school poet meets a young William S. Burroughs look, coupled with his Scottish accented, old man tinged voice. On their latest U.S. tour, we witnessed some fans trying to score free CDs and T-shirts in exchange for lame chapbooks. Ben coolly responded, "I don't read man, I need petrol!" Eat this man's food – he's a visionary, a rebel of course, and a master of eating on the cheap.

Ben offers this recipe off the top of his head as a cheap recipe for hungry people in a hurry.

B. R. (Can't Cook, Insists on Cooking) Wallers' Soup Poutain

INGREDIENTS   *Serves 6*

2 cups basmati rice
1 onion
Sugar, to taste
Salt, to taste
1 tomato
1 tin of baked beans (he's Scottish, now residing in London)
Mild Madras curry powder
1 tin of tuna (again, the U.K. thing)

It's not a soup unless you add extra liquid (e.g., a tin of chopped tomatoes but please Napolina only, it has to be the best for this recipe, Napolina yeah).
As a soup it can also be a sauce for pasta.
As a stew it goes with rice. Here's how to make rice correctly.

PREPARATION

1. Wash the rice. Basmati is best for this recipe. Drain it as much as you can, then add one and a half times water exactly. You should have used a glass to measure the rice that you can tell what's half a glass for the water. If you've fucked it up you should forget it and eat some biscuits ("cookies") or have a drink.
2. So you put the rice on at minimum heat with airtight lid on.

3 When you can hear it crackling it means all the water has been drunk by the rice particles and it's starting to stick to the pan. Don't panic: Turn the heat off and leave it for a few minutes: the residual moisture will unstick the rice from the bottom of the pan if you haven't completely fucked it up by leaving it too long on the heat.

4. Meanwhile, fry the finely chopped onion, adding sugar and salt (my wife's tip).

5. Add the chopped tomatoes.

6. Add everything else. The clash of cultures between baked beans, tuna, and curry powder creates a sweet taste that appeals to one's inner baby.

Butternut Squash Soup

The New Amsterdams? What was wrong with the old one? Nothing, of course, but that doesn't mean there wasn't room for improvement. The New Amsterdams have been offering up their indie-tinged and country-twinged tunes since the dawn of this century. Over time, their music has deepened — laying down its own roots, while forging stronger links to the already existing roots of traditional American music. They consistently draw on the importance of home — whether it be their physical home of Lawrence, Kansas or home as a metaphysical concept, a safe place of refuge in a dangerous world. And what better way to create the experience of home than a hearty bowl of butternut squash soup.

INGREDIENTS   *Serves 6*

2-½ pounds butternut squash
Olive oil
1-½ teaspoons salt
⅛ teaspoon black pepper
Toasted squash seeds for garnish
1 large onion, diced
4 cloves garlic, minced
2 -½ cups plain soy milk

PREPARATION

1. Slice squash in half. Remove seeds and set aside.
2. Brush flesh of squash with olive oil and season with a pinch of salt and a few grinds of black pepper.
3. Place on a baking sheet in a 350°F oven for at least one hour, or until fully roasted. Squash will be done when a knife can be inserted with no effort, similar to mashed potatoes.
4. When squash is finished in the oven set aside to cool for at least half an hour or until cool to the touch. In the meantime make toasted squash seeds.
5. When squash is cool to the touch remove the skin and put the flesh in a food processor.

6. In the soup pot, sweat the onions and garlic in 2 tablespoons of olive oil with salt and pepper, until soft and translucent (about 3 to 5 minutes).
7. Add garlic and onions to food processor with ½ cup of soy milk. Blend mixture until smooth.
8. Transfer mixture to soup pot on medium-low heat.
9. Add remaining soy milk, salt, and pepper. Stir to combine.
10. Heat soup for twenty minutes.
11. Serve with toasted squash seeds and enjoy.

Toasted Squash Seeds

INGREDIENTS

Squash seeds from one 2-½ pound butternut squash
1 teaspoon olive oil
⅛ teaspoon salt
⅛ teaspoon cayenne pepper
½ teaspoon sugar

PREPARATION

1. Remove seeds from squash and wash them off.
2. Toss with olive oil, salt, sugar, and cayenne pepper.
3. Spread on a non-stick baking sheet and roast in a 350°F oven for 10 to 20 minutes.
4. Let cool and serve on top of soup.

Italian Wedding Soup

Sonic Youth – what could we possibly tell you at this point that you don't already know? They buzzed and whirred their way through the No New York era, swooned and soared to their ensuing indie rock stardom, all the while steadfastly averring and guarding the musical avant-garde. Their fame and influence knows no bounds, spawning a legion of detuned guitarists worldwide. They are so big, gas station attendants keep their signed gas receipts as autographed souvenirs. Not that either of us ever did this; it was somebody we, um, know.

But we did not come here to celebrate our love of Sonic Youth, but to celebrate the love to be found in Sonic Youth. If there is one golden rule of band formation it is that featuring romantic partners in your lineup is dangerous – both for the band and for the couple. But Thurston and Kim's marriage stands in distinct contrast, a stirring symbol of what is possible both musically and domestically. So what better way to celebrate their enduring love than with Lee Ranaldo's recipe for Italian Wedding Soup? We can't promise your relationship will last as long or be as successful, but we can promise you a decent meal to get things started. The rest is up to you.

Lee

This is a winter favorite at our house; tasty, nutritious, and delicious. The kids love it and so does everyone else.

INGREDIENTS

Serves 6 to 8

2 to 3 carrots, chopped
1 large onion, diced
2 to 4 (or more!) cloves garlic, chopped
2 quarts chicken stock
½ pound ground veal
½ pound ground beef
2 packages or bunches of spinach
1 pound small pasta of your choice (should
    be smaller than the tiny meatballs but still
    have some substance. I like something like
    ditali but you can use anything. Other nice
    ones are farfallini and orecchietti.)

1 egg
Breadcrumbs
1 teaspoon salt
½ teaspoon black pepper
Olive oil
Parmesan cheese

Preparation

1. Sauté carrots, onion, and garlic cloves until almost brown (about 7 to 9 minutes) in a few tablespoons of extra virgin olive oil.
2. Add 6 to 8 cups stock and simmer 45 minutes to 2 hours.
3. Add salt and pepper to taste while simmering, along with a *bouquet garni* of your choice (rosemary, thyme, sage, etc. + 1 bay leaf). Reserve a bit of stock in case soup boils down too far (keep pot covered but not completely tight).
4. Mix the veal and beef in a bowl.
5. Add 1 egg, breadcrumbs, up to 1 teaspoon salt (don't forget the salt!), and ½ teaspoon black pepper.
6. Roll into tiny meatballs approximately ½-inch in diameter.
7. Sauté until browned and fully cooked although not overdone (they will cook further in the broth). Set aside.
8. Clean the spinach well to remove all sand and grit.
9. Pull out center stalks (this takes a little time) – pull it all the way up through each leaf to get as much of the center stalk out as possible.
10. Sauté the spinach in olive oil (2 to 3 tablespoons) until quite wilted (you may have to do this in 2 to 3 batches).
11. On a cutting board, chop into medium-coarse pieces and set aside.
12. When the soup has been simmering for a good while (30 minutes to 1 hour), use a food processor to puree a good part of the broth. The object here is to get a nice smooth consistency. I usually leave some of the vegetables behind so there is a little floating in the soup, but the general desire is for it to be pretty "broth-y" rather than chock full of veggies like a minestrone.
13. Once the soup has been pureed you can add the meatballs and the spinach, cook another 15 to 30 minutes and you're done.
14. Have the pasta prepared and add to individual bowls (don't cook it in the soup as it will get too soft). Add however much pasta to the soup you like.
15. Serve piping hot with grated Parmesan, more salt and pepper to taste. Yum!

Review of Sonic Youth's Italian Wedding Soup, by George Tabb:

Never EVER eat anything from a band that can't tune their guitars.
The meat is sure to be expired, and the carrots, already used.
If Sonic Youth ever hires real roadies, then try their food.

We first learned of Xiu Xiu from our friend Rob Fisk. Rob, a founding member of Deerhoof, has collaborated a bit with the group. We had known Rob a long time – not through music originally, but through food. Rob worked making pizza in San Francisco and took pity on Lynn's poor unemployed self and helped land him a job making pizza alongside him. But times changed. Just as he was forming Deerhoof, Lynn was leaving town to go back to school. Their paths remained uncrossed for over a decade, until he came through town touring with his new band. After a hard night's sleep on our floor, Rob repaid our generosity with a handful of CDs from his new record label. Nestled among these gems was the work of Xiu Xiu, a genre-defying West Coast-based band that revolves around its one core member, Jamie Stewart. But why are we spinning this yarn, which seems to have so little to do with the specific recipe? Well, it's a block of tofu. What did you want us to say? We suppose we could go on and on about the complexity that sits underneath the surface of this most simple of recipes, which allows it to take on and enhance many flavors and genres. And then we could make some literary leap connecting the food with the band, weaving them so tightly together that you can't see one without the other. But we won't. Because it's a block of tofu. This is how they eat. Enjoy.

Lazy times lunch of Xiu Xiu

INGREDIENTS   *Serves 1*

Tofu

PREPARATION

1. Take a cold block of tofu out of the fridge.
2. Wash it off.
3. Eat it with a fork.
4. Stare out the window.

Fried Roots

Neptune

Hailing from the Boston area, but having much success on their frequent European tours, Neptune started as a sculpture project of guitarist Jason Sanford. The guitars are soldered and massive, the electronics homemade, and the percussion is recycled urban refuse. Fried roots is a brilliant use of pantry soon-to-be refuse, a great way to empty the cupboards, without tasting like that's what you're up to.

Dan

This recipe has been fed to so many bands that have slept on my floor. It's cheap. Serve with black beans seasoned with nutritional yeast, cumin, cinnamon, and tofu scramble.

INGREDIENTS   *Serves 6*

4 or 5 red bliss potatoes
1 to 2 medium or large sweet potatoes
1 to 2 medium-sized beets
1 medium purple onion
6 cloves garlic
3 or 4 green onions
Sprinkle of rosemary
Salt
Black pepper
Cayenne pepper
Paprika
Cumin
Olive oil
Water

PREPARATION

1. In a large frying pan, cover the bottom with water, add a fair amount of olive oil and turn on high. Cut the red bliss potatoes in half, then in slices. Do not peel.

2. Peel the sweet potatoes and beets, cut in half, then in slices.
3. Cut the onion the same way.
4. When the water boils add all the potatoes, onion, and 2 pinches of rosemary. Keep the heat on high and keep adding water as it evaporates, don't add too much but just enough so the potatoes don't burn. Stir frequently.
5. When the potatoes start to soften, cut garlic into long strips and add all spices to your liking. When the potatoes are almost cooked, cut green onions into 1-inch pieces, add and stir. It's good to let it burn a little bit from time to time while cooking.

Lancashire Hot Pot with Dumplings

Genesis P-Orridge

Genesis is legendary, a leader in Industrial music (see Opening Track), so it's quite a surprise that his favorite food is actually that of peasants. One might think he ate some sort of futuristic space food. Eat his food, and if you aren't familiar with Genesis, read up on him/her NOW – essential for any music fan or artist.

Genesis

My favorite meals in the various countries and cultures I have visited always seem to be POOR CUISINE. That is, recipes created by the lowest classes to help meager resources of food stretch as far as possible, even giving an impression of containing more food than they really do. There are other recipes I have read for Lancashire Hot Pot in cookbooks, but this one was initiated by my mother, MIMI MEGSON, after the second World War when some basic food rationing was still in force during my early childhood in Manchester. Many countries have versions of this meal. It's a kind of stew, or goulash designed to use whatever vegetables are in season, leftover bits of meat, and plenty of water to give volume. As the years have passed I have adapted my mother's version to suit my own tastes and so far it has proved popular with friends and my fellow musicians in Psychic TV/PTV3.

Stew

INGREDIENTS

Serves 8

15 cups water
5 pounds potatoes
1-¼ pounds fresh carrots, chopped or slices
1 small cauliflower heart
3 leeks
½ pound Brussels sprouts
1 sweet onion, sliced
½ pound mushrooms, cleaned and broken into chunks
1 pound plum tomatoes, quartered
1 tin of corn beef, cubed
1 cup beef stock
Salt, as desired

Preparation

1. Take a large stockpot and put in 15 cups of filtered water.
2. Peel and then wash clean 5 pounds of potatoes. Make sure to cut out eyes and bruises.
3. Cut the potatoes up into chunks about 1- to 2-inches long by 1-inch thick.
4. Add chopped up potatoes to water in the pan.
5. Peel 1-¼ pounds of fresh carrots and chop them, or slice them into pieces about a ¼ to ½-inch thick.
6. Add carrots to the water and potatoes in the pan.
7. Separate cauliflower head into small florets and add to pan.
8. Take 3 leeks (if they are in season) and cut off only the white end near the roots. Slice off the roots. Then cut 1-inch sections of the leeks and add to the pan.
9. Take ½ pound of Brussels sprouts (when in season) and cut off the top part of the stem, remove outer leaves and cut a cross across the stem. Add these to your pan.
10. Peel off the outer layer of one sweet onion and slice it up. Add this to the contents of your pan.
11. Finally, for this first stage of your meal, add 1 heaped tablespoon of salt.

> Put your pan with the aforementioned ingredients onto your stove and turn on the electric or gas ring half way up.
> While the pan is beginning to cook, keep busy!

12. Take ½ pound standard white mushrooms and scrub them clean in filtered water. Then break them up by hand into roughly 4 to 5 chunks (or pieces if you prefer) and store them on a dish.
13. Take 1 pound of plum tomatoes and remove the nasty ends, then quarter them (just like medieval times!).
14. If you live in England, possibly even in Europe, you can make a stock from either OXO Cubes, or a cup of BISTO. In the U.S. and elsewhere there will be equivalent beef stock products you can substitute. Aim for 1 cup (280 mls) of stock when you are done.

Once your pan is boiling on the stove, leave it cooking for 10 minutes. Turn up the cooking plate if necessary to reach boiling point. Not heavy boiling, nice and bubbly, like volcanic mud. Next, you can add your mushrooms, your stock and your tomatoes.

The two stage cooking process is to try and have all the various ingredients as near to equally cooked as possible at the end.

OKAY! The last ingredient is one tin of corned beef! Yes, really. Get a quality brand. Cut the corned beef up into approximately 1-inch cubes. Add this meat after 15 to 20 minutes depending on how well the potatoes and carrots seem cooked. This last ingredient gives flavor and thickens the hot pot.

Now turn off your stove and make dumplings.

Dumplings

INGREDIENTS

1 cup shortening
2 cups self rising flour

1 cup water (or less)
Salt, as desired

PREPARATION

1. Take 1 cup of shortening. In Europe this would be Atora Suet. In the U.S. it would be Crisco (no naughty jokes here) or there is a great new health food product Earth Balance shortening.
2. Add the shortening to 2 cups of self-rising flour.
3. Add a heaped teaspoon full of salt.
4. Add one slightly less than full cup of water.
5. Using a fork, mix and grind the flour and shortening really well together, while occasionally adding water. Eventually you should have a nice dry-ish clay consistency.
6. Split your dumpling mix into 6 equal amounts and gently make each into a ball. DO NOT squeeze them tight or you will have sinkers!
7. Now turn on the stove/cooker again. Getting the hot pot boiling quickly and drop in the dumplings. Put a lid over the pan.
8. Check the pan carefully. Within 5 minutes your dumplings should float to the surface nice and fluffy and big.

There is enough in this recipe to do two separate servings for four people. The second day the hot pot matures and tastes even better. Keep your pan in the fridge over night. Then make new dumplings, and bring hot pot to a boil. Add dumplings and in 5 minutes you are ready to gorge yourselves again.

Bring it on! NYC's best full on Fun Rock assault clearly know how to party, and are known for excelling at excess. Sure this drink is trashy, but we all know buying alcohol for a crowd is pricey. And who wouldn't rather drink with the gang than sip wine with the stiffs? Take the Bling Kong route and serve your Jangling with pride! Life is not always champagne and roses.

INGREDIENTS   *Serves 1*

---

40 ounces Old English Malt Liquor
Grape soda

PREPARATION

1. Drink 40-ounce Old English Malt Liquor down to the top of the label.
2. Fill the 40-ounce bottle back up with grape soda.
3. Throw away whatever is left of the grape soda.
4. Enjoy contents of 40-ounce bottle!

Beetza

The standards of music as defined by the world of American Bandstand were simple. A song was successful to the extent it could be described by the phrase, "It's got a great beat, and you can dance to it." The A Frames push that standard to a whole new level. This group of Seattle musicians boasts an impeccable pedigree, featuring former members of such groups as the Cows, Butthole Surfers, and Scratch Acid. But what about the music? "You can dance to it, and it's got a great beetza."

Beetza? What in the hell is that? Nothing short of one of the greatest culinary inventions of this young century. The frozen pizza is a double-edged pizza cutter. On the one hand, its low price and low stress preparation makes it a favorite of the underemployed and overworked everywhere. But this same easiness can get old quick. After all, if you are in a situation in which frozen pizza is a central staple of your diet, you are also the sort who might benefit from that little special touch to brighten your day. Don't worry; the A Frames have your back. Take a frozen pizza, any frozen pizza. Take a beet, any beet. Put them together, and you have transformed your pedestrian pizza with a touch of sublime beetitude. And it is not just the taste; marvel at the way the beets bleed purple into the molten cheese. Divine!

Erin

It sounds weird but we have converted many picky eaters into beetza lovers over the years. You can count us among the skeptics – make that former skeptics. This is a nice treat. And the proverbial icing on the cake? The beets stain the cheese a beautiful purple color. A delight for all the senses.

INGREDIENTS   *Serves 4*

1 thin style plain cheese frozen pizza
2 medium-sized beets, cooked and sliced

PREPARATION

1. Take 1 thin style plain cheese frozen pizza (we use these awesome locally made ones that are nice and big and flat).
2. Steam or bake 2 medium-sized beets. Once they are cool slice them thin (¼-inch) and place on frozen pizza.
3. Put the pizza in the oven and bake.

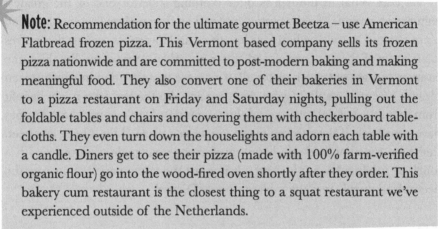

Note: Recommendation for the ultimate gourmet Beetza – use American Flatbread frozen pizza. This Vermont based company sells its frozen pizza nationwide and are committed to post-modern baking and making meaningful food. They also convert one of their bakeries in Vermont to a pizza restaurant on Friday and Saturday nights, pulling out the foldable tables and chairs and covering them with checkerboard table-cloths. They even turn down the houselights and adorn each table with a candle. Diners get to see their pizza (made with 100% farm-verified organic flour) go into the wood-fired oven shortly after they order. This bakery cum restaurant is the closest thing to a squat restaurant we've experienced outside of the Netherlands.

Matt's Ultra Healthy Hot Dog

Japanther

This peanut butter and banana sandwich would have helped keep Elvis alive (or helped kill him, depending on how you look at it). Follow Japanther, and not the King.

INGREDIENTS/PREPARATION

Serves 1

1 banana on
1 piece of whole wheat bread with creamy peanut butter with honey on top of banana (like mustard)

Tomorrow's Friend Drink

Alessandra

This is a simple drink that I've become rather obsessed with on a daily basis and that most of the girls of Tomorrow's Friend have become known for on a personal level. At one point our favorite local record store/café in Greenpoint, Brooklyn, Eat Records, had it on their wall menu named after us which was fun, for lack of a better word. Its health factor is undeniable. I like to joke by calling it the liquid I imagine would drip straight from Mother Earth's Breast.

INGREDIENTS   *Serves 1*

Water
Honey
Milk

PREPARATION

1. Boil water in a pan (if you're on tour or traveling I find it convenient to use the hotel's in room coffee machine! Just remove the filter, pour the water into the machine as if you were making coffee and use the dripped hot water once it's done).
2. Put 1 big tablespoon of honey in a mug.
3. Pour hot water in ¾ to the top.
4. Add a dash of milk.
5. Stir and drink.

Birthday Celebration

Okay...nothing is lamer than blowing off a friend's birthday. There's nothing worse than no one putting effort into your birthday, and it just being any other day — so don't let it happen to others either! You are asking for bad karma if you forget to help celebrate a friend or loved one's birthing day. A gift is required, sure, but a nice home cooked meal complete with a birthday cake is encouraged.

Pick one of the following entrées that you think the birthday boy or girl will most appreciate. And be sure to include the lovely cake from 16 Bitch Pile Up. Birthday parties put everyone in a good mood — not just the guest of honor. People like to give their well wishes and catch up. And maybe someone will get naked and do karaoke. See you again next year.

Valentine's Not Side Salad

Jucifer

Ah, the salad. Too often, home cooks prepare salad as an afterthought, tossing in out-of-season tomatoes and aging celery with whatever limp greens happen to be in the crisper. What a disgrace! Salads can be the high point of the meal, if the chef takes the slightest bit of care. Try Amber's salad, as an entrée or alongside one. Listen to her, she's got "Rock Star" tattooed on her knuckles for god's sakes!

INGREDIENTS
Serves 4

1 head of lettuce
Fresh spinach, as desired
Fresh cilantro, as desired
1 small onion
15-20 baby carrots
Handful of cashews, peanuts, and almonds
1 Granny Smith apple, diced
Handful of dried cranberries

PREPARATION

1. In large bowl wash and tear by hand one head iceberg or any type lettuce.
2. Add fresh spinach and cilantro to taste.
3. Chop small onion and 15-20 baby carrots coarsely and add to lettuce mixture.
4. Add handful of cashews, peanuts, and almonds as preferred or available.
5. Add one Granny Smith apple, diced.
6. Add handful of dried cranberries (Orange flavor Craisins are best).
7. Mix well and enjoy! Best dressed with vinaigrette or fruit-based dressing.

Note: Salad tip – To store greens, layer the leaves between paper towels in a storage container or plastic Ziploc bag for 3 to 4 days. Or, opt for packaged greens, which offer a variety and mix of different lettuces and can keep in the refrigerator (unopened) for up to 2 weeks.

Also, it's essential to dry the greens after washing or else you've got soggy greens! Use a salad spinner if you fancy gadgets; otherwise, drain lettuce in a colander and complete the drying process by wrapping in kitchen towels until any excess water is removed.

Curried Chicken Sriracha
with Couscous

Captured! By Robots

Captured! By Robots are a postmodern band consisting of JBOT (a human) and his robots. A splendid idea to get rid of troublesome band mates!

All (humans) who try this piquant recipe devour it. Even those who typically shy away from spicier food are fond of it. It's a nice one pot meal, with protein and veggies.

JBOT

It's easy, and I live on this stuff. Oh, and as a side I do a little couscous.

INGREDIENTS   *Serves 1*

Olive oil
Butter
1 clove garlic, chopped
Chicken breast
Paprika, salt, curry, and hot sauce, as desired
1 cup white button mushrooms, sliced
1 cup red peppers, sliced
Champagne

PREPARATION

1. Use a skillet on very high heat.
2. Add olive oil, butter, garlic, and the cut-up chicken breast.
3. Add paprika, salt, pepper, a little curry, and that spicy sauce with the rooster on the bottle, it's called Sriracha.
4. Cook until all the outside of the chicken is done, then add mushrooms and red peppers.
5. Don't disturb the pan too much, so the veggies get a good burn on them.
6. When it cooks down, and all is done, deglaze with champagne, and it's awesome!

Fettuccine Carbonara

Chariots are widely regarded as the best punk band in the large music scene in Minneapolis (they were officially crowned "best punk band" by *City Pages*, the city's alternative weekly). They play loud, fast punk featuring the screaming voice of Travis Bog, formerly of the Sons of Zarathustra. They also make a mean pasta dinner, that's just the right combination of festive and filling. Eric of Chariots shares his favorite dish.

INGREDIENTS   *Serves 4*

Fettuccine noodles
Chopped bacon
1 part cream
1 part sweet cream butter
2 cups grated Parmesan cheese
2 cloves garlic, minced
Sweet peas
Salt and pepper, to taste

PREPARATION

1. First, bring a large pot of water to a boil. Add the fettuccine and cook for 8 to 10 minutes or until al dente.
2. Drain it and set aside.
3. Then bring out the bacon and fry it up in a pan over medium heat until it gets nice and crispy. Set it on a paper towel to drain off all the excess fat.
4. Cut it up into smaller pieces and set aside.
5. Mix the cream, butter, and cheese together in a bowl.
6. Then add the bacon, garlic, and peas. Pour the entire concoction over the pasta in a pan and cook it for a minute or two over low heat to thicken up the sauce.
7. Salt and pepper to taste and then serve.

Finn's Sopranoziti

This Sonic Unyon label band features sound manipulator Dale Flattum (artist and former member of Steel Pole Bathtub and Milkcut). Dale's developed a graphic icon: the Tooth Squatch. If you see a comic-like smiling tooth on stickers or flyers around town, you can be sure that Mr. Flattum posted it. We are proud to say we have a Tooth Squatch painting in our dining room. If the rumors are true, it is one that started the entire craze.

This dish has lots of ingredients, sure, but all the components build on each other to create an incredible flavor punch. This recipe will give you new love for boring old pasta. And, it shows you care.

Finn's Sopranoziti is to be eaten while watching your favorite season of *The Sopranos* on DVD.

INGREDIENTS   *Serves 6*

3 tablespoons olive oil
1 chopped yellow onion
1 diced red bell pepper
2 teaspoons basil
1 teaspoon oregano
1 teaspoon thyme
1½ teaspoons salt
1 can of tomatoes (28 ounces)
6 ounces tomato paste
1 tablespoon honey
One bottle of red wine, preferably something you'd be willing to drink
2 bay leaves
½ pound sweet or spicy Italian sausage
5 cloves garlic
Black pepper
1 pound penne
2 tablespoons butter
1 pound mozzarella
1 container ricotta
Fresh Parmesan cheese

PREPARATION

1. Chop the onion and pepper together, then sauté in the olive oil with the salt and herbs for about ten minutes.
2. Dump the tomatoes and tomato paste in, and add the honey with the same tablespoon used for the olive oil (it'll roll right off the spoon if you leave the remnants of the oil on there).
3. Pour a generous amount of the wine in there, then grind a lot of pepper, drop the bay leaves in, cover the pot, and let it cook on low heat for about 30 minutes.
4. While this is going on, fry the sausages and then put them in the sauce.
5. Add some more wine and some more black pepper, then cover again (do this every 10 minutes). Chop the garlic with a knife – don't use a garlic press – into very fine little pieces, then throw it in after the sauce has been heating for 30 minutes. Cook for another 10 minutes.
6. While the sauce is cooking, boil water and cook the penne.
7. Grate the mozzarella.
8. When the penne is done, drain it, then cut about 2 tablespoons of butter and put it in the same pot the penne was cooked in.
9. Stir it all, then pour the sauce, the mozzarella, and the ricotta in as well. Make sure the burner is on very low while this is going on to keep everything hot. This is going to look very gross and make gross sounds while stirring, but disregard the grossness. Pour the whole mixture into a casserole dish and bake at 350°F for 30 to 40 minutes, depending on what sort of consistency you want.

When cooking rice pasta, keep a very close eye on it, because it cooks faster than wheat pasta, and the last thing you want in your ziti is mushy pasta. It should only take about 6 minutes, maybe less, to cook rice penne. Also, keep in mind that if you do use real pork sausage, some places do use breadcrumbs to hold the sausages together, so if you have a wheat allergy the sausage will bug you.

Note 1: The wine and honey are the main essentials, because they add a sweetness to the flavor. Use fresh herbs when possible, and don't skimp on the black pepper. You can't use enough, really.

Finn Cohen

My girlfriend has a gluten allergy, so when I make this for her I use rice penne, but only the Pasta Joy brand, because all the other rice pastas suck.

Birthday Cundt Cake

Sarah and her band mates made this anatomically correct version of a battered torso birthday cake for birthday boy Greh of Condritic Sound Records. The band transported the cake to the party in near 100 degree weather, from Columbus to Detroit (4 hours) in their non-AC equipped van. They put it in a huge Tupperware container full of ice (that melted almost immediately). The cake still manages to look fabulous, even if the icing appears a little bit celulitious! The cake, which marries beautiful flowers and well executed art with somewhat violent destruction, is an appropriate description of their music as well.

INGREDIENTS   *Serves 16 to 20*

Cake

> 4 boxes of red cake mix
> 4 boxes of marble cake mix
> 2 cups powdered sugar
> 2 cups water

Frosting

> 3 cans strawberry whipped icing
> 4 cans cream cheese whipped icing
> 2 cans dark fudge whipped icing
> 1 teaspoon orange food coloring
> Splash of orange juice

Decorating

> 1 package of red licorice strips
> 1 bar dark chocolate
> 1 butcher knife
> 1 tube red gel

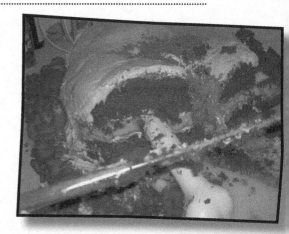

Cundt Cake, photo courtesy of Sarah Bernat

Photo courtesy of Sarah Bernat,
16 Bitch Pile Up

PREPARATION

1. Bake red cakes and marble cakes separately according to directions on box, use 9 x 9 or 9 x 12 cake pans.
2. Allow cakes to cool completely, cut cakes into approximately 4- to 6-inch pieces and form the pieces into torso, hip, pelvic and thigh shapes (your discretion).
3. Mix powdered sugar and water, use mixture to adhere cake pieces together, glaze entire cake with mixture.
4. If you have some plastic bones, build the torso and thigh shapes around the bones.
5. Put the formed cake in freezer for 10 to 20 minutes to harden.
6. Separate the licorice strips and insert around bones for tendony/veiny appearance (your discretion).
7. Mix the strawberry, cream cheese, and dark fudge whipped icings to a smooth, flesh colored mixture.
8. Add orange food coloring and splash of orange juice, mix thoroughly.
9. Spread liberally over torso, hips, pelvis, and thighs, but do not cover the ends (thighs and waist) so as to let the red and marble cake show through. Smooth to a skin-like quality.
10. Put in freezer to harden.
11. Use a grater to shave the chocolate bar into shredded pieces, and sprinkle over pelvis for the appearance of pubic hair.
12. Insert butcher knife between thighs into pelvis.
13. Squeeze red gel around "knife wound" and around the area (your discretion).
14. Decorate with real or fake flowers and serve immediately.
15. Eat with your hands!

No Fond Food Memories of Your Own? Borrow These.

We admit it. We're a little jealous of people who come from strong cooking backgrounds, who have an old family recipe for just about anything, who remember an old world baking secret they learned from their great aunt Sally, who grew up in a house that was always filled with the sounds and smells of people coming together to make food. Neither of us had that. Specifically, Kay's family was just another white-bread suburban family, where the white bread was not wonderful, but simply Wonder. Her deepest family food memory is not exactly the stuff of heart-warming tradition. When she was in school, Kay's mom was supposed to make enough cupcakes for the entire class to feast on during one of the various elementary school events we suffered through as children. After dutifully completing the cupcakes, she suddenly was struck with a moment of dread. "What if I made these wrong, and instead of a festive fifth-grade function, we have a miniature killing fields, with children keeling over from poisoned treats?" Well, that was that. The cupcakes went directly into the trash bin. Yes, Kay's classmates were disappointed to be denied their treats, but do you think they would have been happier in a box pushing up daisies. Maybe poor Natalia, but the rest of them don't know how lucky they were barely dodging that bullet. Don't expect to find the recipe for these cupcakes in this, or any other, cookbook. The poison is a secret family recipe.

Maybe you don't have any family traditions of your own either. Or maybe you do, but you are looking for some additional comfort food in your life. Or maybe you just want a little peak into the family history of some of your favorite musicians. Whatever your motivations, you will find something to your liking here.

Ma Vig's Pasta Sauce

Lynn once spent a summer living in Dresden, Germany. He was in the Old City, which was ironically filled with new buildings, because of the devastating bombing campaign the city suffered during World War II. Thus, he spent his days living in a soul-less communist-bloc era apartment block, staring out the window across the Elbe River at the beautiful old buildings in the New City. Lynn felt a level of alienation – caught within the landscape of competing ravages of the past and cut off from the promises of the city trying to come to terms with its checkered past and its unknown future.

We once spent a summer living in the Dresden Dolls. We heard in them an alienation, not unlike the one Lynn had experienced in the city of Dresden, the product of incommensurable forces crashing together. This Boston duo pulls from the musical traditions of cabaret and punk, employing youth ennui to expose and espouse the twisted fate of the world, and always fall into laughter to keep from crying. The alienation starts at home, with songs of broken families premised on broken promises. That's why it was so surprising when drummer Brian Viglione sent us Mama Vig's Pasta Sauce, shattering the image of dysfunctional families and cold, mute stares across the dinner table, where everyone choked down the food as a means to choking back the tears. But we should expect nothing less than another virtuoso performance from these cabaret artists – but the question still remains, which one is the act?

An important lesson for all home cooks: The addition of cinnamon to pasta sauces (and other savory dishes) yields complex and intense flavors usually associated with restaurant quality fare. Cinnamon, which was once valued at three times the price of silver, should be a staple in your kitchen, and not just for the sweet stuff.

Brian

This is the traditional family sauce that my father grew up on and that he and my mother cooked for us when I was young. It wasn't until I was living on my own and cooking for myself that I began to long for the comforting, home-cooked flavor that I remembered, that all the store bought sauces were lacking. I called my grandmother to get the recipe and soon realized that it was the cinnamon that gave this sauce its distinctive flavor. Now, it's hard for me to go back and I usually wind up making a batch and leaving it in the fridge to use throughout the week!

There are a few variations of this sauce that I use as well, which include adding sliced, baby Portobello mushrooms, sautéed with a pinch of garlic salt, substituting the black olives with raisins, which add a sweet, tender texture to the sauce. Or on Christmas Eve, it was tradition to use anchovies in place of the olives, pignoli nuts and raisins. Personally, I have respectfully laid this tradition aside, as I am not a huge fan of anchovies, but felt it should be noted for this book. The cooking time, for the most part, depends on if you choose to include meat or not. The longer you let it simmer, the more the flavors are drawn out. However, I usually make mine without the meat and get the sauce all going on the stove first, then begin to prepare the pasta (tortellini!) and the rest of the meal. By the time everything else is ready and the table is set, we're good to go. Whip up some sautéed kale or grilled asparagus with minced garlic and lemon, a loaf of crusty bread, and you've got yourself a classic "welcome-home-from-tour, now-shaddup-n-eat" Brian Viglione speciale for you and your gumbas! Salute!

INGREDIENTS   *Serves 6 with pasta*

1 can tomato paste
1 can tomato sauce
1 can whole peeled tomatoes
1 teaspoon basil
2 bay leaves
1 tablespoon parsley
1 teaspoon cinnamon
1 to 2 tablespoons sugar
½ teaspoon salt
½ teaspoon ground black pepper
Black olives
Pignoli nuts, browned in a sauté pan
* 1 pound ground beef or sausage, browned

* optional

PREPARATION

Combine and simmer for 35 minutes to 2 hours.

Mud Cookies

Daniel Johnston

Daniel does not have access to email, nor is he much of a cook (which apparently had no bearing on his tenure at an Austin, Texas McDonald's in the mid 1980s). Luckily his brother, Dick, offered us this recipe. Apparently, Daniel does have some food preferences other than his slave-like devotion to Mountain Dew. This is Daniel and Dick's favorite snack recipe while growing up, which they referred to as "mud cookies" – you may know them as no-bake peanut butter oatmeal cookies.

INGREDIENTS   *Makes 2 dozen cookies*

1 stick margarine
$^1/_3$ cup cocoa
$^2/_3$ cup milk
2 cups sugar
$^1/_2$ cup peanut butter
3 cups oatmeal
1 teaspoon vanilla

PREPARATION

1. Melt the margarine in a deep stovetop pan large enough for mixing all the ingredients.
2. Remove from the heat and immediately add the cocoa. Mix until dissolved.
3. Add milk and sugar and return to full heat and stir until dissolved.
4. Bring to a full boil for 2-$^1/_2$ minutes and add the peanut butter. Mix until dissolved.
5. Remove from the heat. Add oatmeal and vanilla and stir until mixed.
6. Spoon onto wax paper, then wait until cool and serve.

Shrimps Della Mamma

Alessandra

My three passions in life are indisputably making music, eating, and hanging around naked with another naked body. Since the first and third ones accordingly have many highs and lows, food takes the cake every time. My winner above all for its consistency in far depths, and always giving with uncharted surprises. I grew up in Rome, Italy and needless to say have always had a four star chef at my fingertips, only a phone call away these days, in the form of my mother: Rita Iavarone. Once in a blue moon I've taken some of the faster and humbly easier recipes away with me and thought it best to share one of those favorites with you. The one I've chosen is a perfect addition for all occasions that can be added to any already prepared menu. It makes me feel good to bring something to the table in return for a nice invitation.

INGREDIENTS

Serves 4

1 purple onion
½ stick of non-salted butter
2 cups of Pinot Grigio white wine
2 dozen raw unfrozen shrimp
Flour
Pure salt and pepper
1 lemon

PREPARATION

1. Finely chop your onion.
2. In a large pan, place butter and chopped onions on a low flame until onions turn brown.
3. While that's going on peel the shells off your shrimps and put them in a large bowl, add salt and pepper.
4. Pour a thick coat of flour onto a flat plate, then take shrimps one by one out of the bowl and into the plate of flour, coating both sides of the shrimp lightly. Then lay them down individually in the pan.

5. Once you have done this to all your shrimps and they are gathered side by side in the pan let them cook for a few minutes (3 or 4 minutes) on low flame still.
6. Now comes my favorite part. I'm a simple person of simple joys: turn them over.
7. Immediately take one cup of the white wine and pour it in the pan all over the shrimp. Watch out for the wine mushroom cloud, but smell its beauty.
8. Cover and let cook for another 5 to 7 minutes (on the sixth minute repeat wine move with your second cup).
9. Cut one big juicy lemon in half, place on either side of plate of shrimps and serve.

Photo by Maximilla Lukacs

Photo by Olivia Wyatt

Grandma's Casserole

You may not think you know the Willowz, but chances are you probably do. Even if you are not up on all the newest bands, you probably take in a movie every once and a while. Rather than go for the standard Hollywood pap smear, your tastes may run more towards the odd and surreal, such as the work of Michel Gondry, director of *Eternal Sunshine of the Spotless Mind* and *The Science of Sleep*, which capture how fantasy and imagination can help you escape even the drabbest life. If you have seen these films, then you have heard the Willowz, who contributed to both soundtracks.

This should come as no surprise – after all, they hail from the "Happiest Place on Earth," Anaheim, California, the home of Disneyland and the larger infrastructure of corporate fantasy. The Willowz are talented enough to heave escaped the clutches of having to work in the dead end service industry in their hometown, but Kay can't count herself so lucky. Growing up in Anaheim's East Coast ugly twin sister city, Orlando, Florida, Kay spent a summer hawking Shamu plushes to the fawning and frightening crowds. Maintaining the fantasy under such conditions can leave one drained and hungry at the end of the day. Shamu might have been content with a bucket of fish, but Kay, and all her fellow service work proles out there, deserve and demand something better. What you need, my friend, is a good casserole recipe. Renowned for their convenience, casseroles can be made ahead, when you've got some time, and then baked later for some yummy goodness, and well needed comforting. And the fact that this is a family recipe just makes it that much homier. Happy days are here again.

This is bass player Jessica Reynoza's family recipe.

INGREDIENTS   *Serves 6*

- 1 pound ground beef
- 1 bunch of green onions
- 8 ounces sour cream
- 1 small can tomato sauce (8 ounces)
- 1 small package of egg noodles
- 1 block of Velveeta cheese (8 ounces)

PREPARATION

1. Brown ground beef and chopped green onions in pan.
2. Drain grease and then add tomato sauce and sour cream to the beef.
3. Mix and simmer for 5 minutes.
4. Follow cooking directions on egg noodle package for cooking the noodles.
5. When finished, pour noodles into a 9 x 12 casserole pan.
6. Then pour meat mixture over the noodles.
7. Grate Velveeta cheese and put on top of the meat and noodles.
8. Cook at 350°F for 30 minutes or until cheese bubbles.

Kate Kannibal's Grandma's Cheesy Spaghetti Hoops

The Priscillas

The U.K. phenomenon that is The Priscillas is equal parts 1950s pinup-style and old school punk rock. They offer this family recipe, which is straight up 1950s dinner fare.

Mandatory: Serve this cheesy deliciousness with an iceberg lettuce wedge drizzled with diced tomatoes and blue cheese dressing. And if you are up for a dessert, a parfait glass full of Chubby Hubby ice cream.

INGREDIENTS   *Serves 4*

Some butter
Some flour
1 pint of milk
Lump of strong cheddar cheese, grated
1 can of spaghetti hoops (Haunted House will do)
Pepper
1 teaspoon oregano
Some breadcrumbs
Ready salted crisps U.K. (or potato chips in America)

PREPARATION

1. Preheat your oven to 400°F.
2. Melt a lump of butter in a pan. When it's hot, put some flour in.
3. Cook it up until it's a bit brown.
4. Slowly add the milk to make a lovely smooth white sauce. Add most of the cheese. Mmmm!
5. Open the can of spaghetti hoops, and stir them in.
6. Add some pepper and oregano.
7. Transfer to an ovenproof dish. Top with breadcrumbs and your leftover cheese. Bake for 20 minutes.
8. Put crisps into the oven to heat.
9. Bake for a further 5 minutes. Serve hot!

Cauliflower with Breadcrumbs

(Grandmother's Way) Captured! By Robots

JBOT's grandmother used to serve up this yummy veggie dish on request. No information is available about the eating habits of the robots' families.

INGREDIENTS   *Serves 4 to 6*

1 head of cauliflower
Breadcrumbs
Butter

PREPARATION

1. Steam one head of cauliflower until you can cut it easily with a spoon.
2. Then put some breadcrumbs in a skillet with a bunch of butter, and toast them. It's tricky, don't burn them, just get them nice and toasty.
3. Then serve breadcrumbs on the side of each serving of cauliflower. The person eating puts their own crumbs on, as you don't want to serve it like that, the breadcrumbs can get mushy.

West Virginia Childhood Popcorn

Shy Child

We all first met back at Wesleyan University. Pete Cafarella and Nate Smith met there as students before eventually moving to the Big City and forming the synth-rock duo Shy Child. Lynn was introduced to them (the band, not the individuals) while also at Wesleyan, although years after they had left, and as a visiting professor, not as a student. While they are forward looking in their sound (as well as forward sounding in their look), they are not afraid to pay homage to the glories of the days gone by, whether that be in their tireless efforts to revive that most versatile of 1980s musical instruments, the keytar (or is it a guiboard?), or in their strong ties to their memories of youth, as evidenced in their recipe for West Virginia Childhood Popcorn. So, as the lights go down, pull out a bowl of their popcorn, and with one eye facing the past and the other the future, enjoy the show.

Nate

I am not much of a cook, but I have a very simple recipe for delicious popcorn that I've been making since I was a kid in West Virginia.

INGREDIENTS   *Serves 1*

½ cup popped corn (stovetop or air popped, not microwave)
¼ stick melted butter
3 to 4 tablespoons brewer's yeast (sometimes called nutritional yeast)
A few shakes of Spike seasoning (a spice blend usually sold in health food stores)

PREPARATION

Shake it up in a bag or a covered bowl, and that's it.

Note: Brewer's/nutritional yeast comes in two forms – flake and powder. The flaky kind is essential for this recipe; the powdered kind has a completely different texture and flavor and is decidedly inferior. The powder is usually sold in large jars, while the flaky kind is most often scooped out of large vats in the health food store.

Lunch Box Redux

Most say that breakfast is the most important meal of the day, but lunch may be the most anticipated. On the job or at school, lunch is the meal we anxiously await to break up the day and have a rest. If you are like most people, you aren't great at pre-planning and often overlook preparing a satisfying midday meal. This is a mistake! Without your own home cooking, you are going to spend a lot more money out at some mediocre sandwich joint with little to no ambience. And, you might even be tempted to fast food it, which we all know is a huge mistake for both dietary and humanitarian reasons.

So, the secret is to plan ahead – and try new things to keep your interest. Don't fall prey to Lean Cuisine or Weight Watchers frozen meals, which are bland and low calorie for a reason – they don't contain much food!! Get a cute Asian-stacked metal lunchbox (the ones with multiple layers for different dishes) and try out the following recipes. Swing your lunchbox or brown bag with pride and treat yourself! Throw in one of the half cans of beers if you must, or an airplane sized Bordeaux. Pack a linen napkin. Lunch is about refueling both your body and your mind so, do it with style.

Bob's Chinese Spicy Cold Celery

Silver Jews

This celery is a nice alternative to a green lettuce salad. If making a composed salad plate, this pairs well with traditional Japanese cucumbers marinated in sugar and vinegar, along with a piece of fish or Asian marinated chicken.

INGREDIENTS

Serves 6 to 8 as a side dish

- 1 pound celery cut in 2-inch strips
- 1 teaspoon salt
- 1 tablespoon plus 1 teaspoon sugar
- 3 tablespoons dark sesame oil
- 1 tablespoon soy sauce
- 2 teaspoons apple cider vinegar
- 1 clove garlic, minced
- Dash of crushed red pepper

PREPARATION

1. Mix celery with salt and 1 teaspoon of sugar, then set aside.
2. Whisk together all other ingredients to make the dressing.
3. Rinse, drain, and pat dry celery, and toss with dressing.
4. Let stand in refrigerator 3 plus hours. Serve chilled.

Silver Jews in Tel Aviv
Photo courtesy of Silver Jews

Bremen Broccoli Cheese Soup

The German Art Students

When a band hails from Madison, Wisconsin, it's a safe bet that their recipe box arsenal contains at least one good cold weather soup. This broccoli cheese delight soothes you when you need it (think a creamier replacement for chicken soup). It was originally potato cheese soup, but since Randy Ballwawn's wife is allergic to potatoes, he adapted it a bit. If you aren't allergic to potatoes, go ahead and toss them in!

INGREDIENTS   *Serves 6*

2 medium onions, chopped
2 tablespoons vegetable oil
1 good-sized bunch of broccoli, chopped
1 cup carrots, chopped
1 teaspoon ground black pepper
Pinch of tumeric
4 cups vegetable stock, chicken stock, or water, your choice
2 cups cream cheese (16 ounces)
2 cups milk
2 cups grated cheddar cheese

PREPARATION

1. Sauté onions in oil for approximately 5 minutes.
2. Stir in broccoli, carrots, pepper, and tumeric.
3. Add stock or water and simmer 15 to 20 minutes until vegetables are soft.
4. Blend cream cheese and milk. Stir into soup.
5. Add cheddar cheese. Reheat. Salt to taste.

Brown Rice Mush

Demolition Doll Rods

Demolition Doll Rods are an infectious band from Detroit ROCK CITY, who everyone loves live because their shows are raucous explosions of the garage-y, fun music (plus they often get naked). They are an all girl band (well, the one guy is in drag), and they live a healthy rock and roll lifestyle (all members are vegans). The In the Red website notes they "happily consume lotus root, kale, millet while they adamantly shun deadly nightshade family members eggplant, green and red peppers, tomatoes and potatoes. They enthusiastically endorse Smooth Move, herbal laxatives."

And for the old school punk rock foodies out there, they've even enjoyed Thanksgiving dinner with The Cramps.

Danny Doll Rod

Here's my specialty, Brown Rice Mush. This isn't much of a recipe, but it's pretty much what I live on.

Ingredients   *Serves 1*

Brown rice (amount depending on serving size)

Olive oil

Nutritional yeast

Bragg's Liquid Aminos

Hot sauce

Preparation

1. Pressure cook some brown rice. It's better pressure cooked, it comes out moist and chewy and takes half the time it would take to boil it.
2. Put some of the brown rice in a bowl, as much as you feel like eating.
3. Pour some good quality olive oil on it, Spectrum Organic Mediterranean Olive Oil is my favorite right now. Then pour some nutritional yeast on it, this is sort of a cheese substitute. It comes in the form of small flakes and it's full of vitamin B. You can get it at any good health food store.
4. Ok, then you put a bit of Bragg's Liquid Aminos on it, a little goes a long way. This stuff is kind of like soy sauce but better. Again any good health food store should have it.
5. Okay, then the last ingredient is hot sauce. I use a brand called Must Bee, that's my favorite, but I think you can only get that one in Detroit. Frank's Red Hot is pretty much the same. So just put a few squirts of hot sauce on there and stir it up and voilà! Tasty mush. Quick, easy, cheap, and nutritious.

The Furious George Sandwich

George Tabb

George Tabb is punk rock royalty – rocking and writing his way throughout the history and history books of the scene. Despite his lofty status, George and Lynn have a lot in common. Both spent their formative years in the not terribly lovely and even less lively Tallahassee, Florida. They were both educated at Leon High School, a distinction they share with Faye Dunaway. George has been called the Professor of Punk by none other than Joey Ramone. Lynn has been referred to as the punk professor by none other than Kay. It almost seems like they have lived the same life, but wait, there's more. Both George and Lynn love sandwiches. And whether you love sandwiches or not (and how couldn't you?), you will still find his recipe tough to resist.

Familiar ingredients are awakened by the unexpected addition of a banana. This sandwich begs for a side of potato chips, rippled please!

INGREDIENTS   *Serves 1*

1 hero roll	Sliced tomato
2 tablespoons mayonnaise	Swiss cheese
1 thinly sliced banana	Sliced onion
Shredded lettuce	Salt and pepper

PREPARATION

1. Cut roll in half and spread mayonnaise evenly over both slices of said bread. Add a little extra to the top bun.
2. Now, take your thinly sliced banana and apply gently to mayo on top roll, planting the fruit deep in the wet thick white substance. Make sure banana is ripe or pre-evaporation of juices may occur.
3. Gently cover with lettuce.
4. Plant tomato slices on lower bun and cover well with Swiss cheese. Make sure tomato is snug in the warmth of the cheese, as well as lubricated from mayo.
5. Sprinkle salt and pepper and add onion. Put together, cut in half, and eat like a monkey. If made wrong, you are allowed to spank yourself.

Tofu Scramble and Tortillas

Calexico

This Tuscon, Arizona band can be found on Touch & Go, and have been kicking it since 1996. Their sound is always evolving but generally includes some fusion of folk, country, mariachi, jazz, and electronica. The band's founding members were originally in Giant Sand, and over the years they've recorded with many, many musicians, including Nancy Sinatra and Neko Case.

This is for those who aren't quite so hardcore as to eat tofu straight off the vine, and prefer it a little more jazzed up.

Photo by Martin Wenk

INGREDIENTS   *Serves 1*

Firm tofu	Garlic
Yellow onion	Flour tortillas
Yellow squash	Salsa
Zucchini	Soy sauce
Mushrooms	Goddess Tahini dressing

PREPARATION

1. Cut tofu into small cubes.
2. Cut veggies.
3. Sauté both tofu cubes and cut onion in a skillet until lightly browned.
4. Add cut veggies and garlic.
5. Serve with warmed flour tortillas and salsa; use a little soy sauce if needed for taste and always bust out the Goddess Tahini dressing.

Note: Add 1 to 2 teaspoons of cumin and/or paprika to the tofu to increase the flavor of this dish.

EZ Pudding

A three ingredient recipe from San Diego favorites, Holy Molar. This recipe is incredibly healthy, yet super rich. An easy snack to whip up, it doesn't dirty anything besides your blender. Plus, every lunch box needs a pudding. Your teeth (not just molars, but also incisors, canines, and bicuspids) will thank you.

INGREDIENTS   *Serves 1*

1 cup maple syrup or 1-½ cups of dates
2 medium avocados
½ cup carob powder

PREPARATION

Combine all ingredients into a blender until smooth. There you have it!

Breaking Bread II: Electric Boogaloo

When people ask Lynn what his biggest influence is, he invariably answers, Bread. Bread? You mean the early 70s soft rock band that coined such hits as "If" and "Make it with you"? No, he means exactly what he said. He means bread, the food made by bringing flour, water, and (usually) salt together, often throwing in a leavening agent like yeast, and then baked, steamed, or fried. Bread: the staff of life. Or, is that the stuff of life? We can't remember, but it doesn't matter, they're both true. Lynn, dear friends, is a breadaholic, but there are no 12 steps that can wean him off the stuff. Not that he plans to ever give it up, thank you very much. Dr. Atkins and his miserable diet are an affront to the deeply engrained values Lynn stands for. For all we care, he can slip on a sidewalk and drop dead. The only consolation with the carb-free craze that swept the nation was the shelves and shelves of beautiful bread left behind for Lynn to devour. But he doesn't want to hog it all to himself. Bread, after all, is for sharing.

Although they both happen in the very same kitchen, do not mistake baking for its relative, cooking. While cooking is an art, baking is a science (not that these are really as different as most people believe – but bear with us while we make a point). While you can feel free to fiddle with the measurements when cooking, be a bit more careful when baking. Still, that's no reason to deny yourself the pleasures of baking. Some people fear making bread – worried by the erratic reputation of yeast. Nonsense! Yeast is a strange and rare beast, to be sure, but with some patience and know-how, it can be tamed. But if you are really put-off (or simply looking for a change), god created easy breads. So now you have no excuse. So what are you waiting for? Preheat that oven and get baking. And don't worry about doing anything wrong, because it is only when you are breaking bread that things are really working.

Jessica's Banana Bread

The Night Porter

The Night Porter is the name of a 1970s film featuring Charlotte Rampling and Dirk Bogarde that deals with Nazis, concentration camps, and sadomasochism. It was the kind of movie that was de rigueur with all the arty and artful kids. The Night Porter is also the name of a band featuring Carla Bozulich and Jessica Catron, whose music deals with rock, rocks, and rocking. They share their recipe for banana bread, the type of recipe that is sure to become de rigueur with people everywhere who eat.

INGREDIENTS

Makes 2 loaves

6 bananas
2 cups sugar
1 cup margarine
4 eggs, well beaten
2-½ cups flour
1 teaspoon salt
2 teaspoons baking soda

PREPARATION

1. Peel and slice bananas.
2. Combine with rest of ingredients. Blend until smooth.
3. Put in 2 greased loaf pans and bake at 350°F for 55 minutes. You can insert a toothpick in the middle, if it comes out clean, it's ready!

Millionaire's Shortbread

Sunset Rubdown, once considered a side project of Spencer Krug's Wolf Parade, no longer live in the shadow of any band or anyone, gaining critical and commercial indie success. Founding member Camilla Wynne, formerly of Pony Up, is a culinary and musical force to be reckoned with, and was instrumental in the writing of this book. Always helpful, informative, and supportive, Camilla was pulling for this book before the first page was even written. And you don't need us to tell you that her recipe is amazing.

Camilla

I am a pastry school graduate, now unemployed pastry chef. I've worked with a few of the big guns in the culinary world, but I just keep quitting to go on tour. Outside of work I prefer to make simpler confections, like Millionaire's Shortbread, my grandmother's recipe. Then I bring them to the boys at band practice because I don't think they feed themselves often enough. They seem to appreciate it.

INGREDIENTS   *Serves 6 to 8*

1 cup all-purpose flour
Pinch of salt
¼ cup sugar
1 cup cold unsalted butter, ½ cup cubed and ½ cup to be melted
⅔ cup brown sugar
2 tablespoons golden syrup or dark corn syrup
1 tin sweetened condensed milk
1 teaspoon vanilla extract
4 ounces bittersweet chocolate
1 teaspoon vegetable oil

PREPARATION

1. Sift together 1 cup all-purpose flour, pinch of salt, and ¼ cup sugar.
2. Rub in ½ cup cold unsalted butter, cut into small pieces.
3. Press into an 8 x 8 tin. Bake in a 350°F oven for 25 minutes, until golden brown. Cool on a wire rack.
4. Combine in a medium saucepan ½ cup unsalted butter, ⅔ cup brown sugar, 2 tablespoons golden syrup or dark corn syrup, and 1 tin sweetened condensed milk.
5. Stir over very gentle heat until sugar dissolves.
6. Increase heat to med-low and bring to a boil.
7. Simmer gently 7 minutes, stirring continuously, until caramel-colored.
8. Add 1 teaspoon vanilla and pour onto shortbread base.
9. Leave to cool and set.
10. Gently melt 4 ounces bittersweet chocolate with 1 teaspoon vegetable oil in a metal bowl set over a pan of simmering water.
11. Spread over caramel.
12. Cut when chocolate is set.

Drawing by Jordan Robson Cramer

"Good" Morning Bread

Trachtenburg Family Slideshow Players

Jason

I originally nicked the basis of/for this recipe off of the back of a rice milk carton. They were possibly calling it "oaty-apple muffins" or something like that. I would often find myself walking around the East Village or the Lower East Side, peering into the windows of bakeries, looking at some brownish and probably a little sweetish-baked bread loaves.

In theory and in practice, the bakeries then slice these loaves into slices and then sell said slices for $2.50-3.00 per slice. With ingredients usually consisting of white flour and white sugar, grocery stores also sell pre-packaged versions of similar loaf slices. Airtight plastic wrapped and laced with chemicals in order to preserve for up to two years, these bread slices are a modern day conglomeration of questionable culinary chemicals. In other words, we are presented with inferior conventionally processed chemical cakes at 200-500% mark up.

What to do? I had to bake these cake/bread loaves myself with the healthiest ingredients available. For a fraction of the price and an insurmountable improvement over the ingredients, these loaves are there for the baking. Follow, or don't follow this recipe. Cooking, like any art form, is an extension of life. It is always open for interpretation and improvisation on the original, then, that in turn, makes you (and your art) the new original.

INGREDIENTS (USE ALL ORGANIC)   *Makes 1 loaf*

1-½ cups spelt flour
¾ cup rolled oats
1 cup rice milk
½ cup agave nectar syrup (or a little less)
1 teaspoon baking powder
1-¼ teaspoons cinnamon
½ teaspoon nutmeg
½ teaspoon sea salt

1. Mix all ingredients in a bowl.
2. Pour into a lightly greased and floured pan.
3. Bake at 375°F for 15 to 20 minutes, or until cooked through.

Note 1: You can also use a toaster oven if the regular oven doesn't work – like ours.

Note 2: This bread, eaten in a rental car, can cost you $25 to $50 (for the clean up charge associated with the crumbs). The Trachtenburg Family knows this from personal experience.

Alastair's Italian White Country Bread

Sponge

INGREDIENTS

Makes 2 loaves

1 cup strong white bread flour
¼ ounce yeast
1 cup warm water (blood temperature)

PREPARATION

1. Put warm water in a large mixing bowl, sprinkle yeast over top, mix till it looks cloudy, milky.
2. Add the flour, mix together with wire whisk, cover mixture with cling film, or what is called saran wrap to you. Leave in a warm place for at least three hours, up to three days. The longer left, the stronger the flavor the bread will have. If keeping the sponge for more than three days, put it in the fridge!

Bread

INGREDIENTS

3-½ cups strong white flour
1 cup whole meal flour
2 teaspoons of salt (I like to use a sea salt ground down in a pestle)
1 cup water (blood temperature)

PREPARATION

1. Put all dry ingredients together, add your sponge to this. Then add the water a bit at a time. As you are going for a feel of the dough and all flours act different, you may need more or less. The feel you want is smooth, soft, and elastic.
2. Mix this all together in the bowl, I use a bread hook to knead the bread. If you don't have one, you'll have to do this by hand. On a clean, smooth counter top, sprinkle with flour, and flour your hands. Turn contents of bowl out onto counter, knead for at least 5 minutes, till the dough turns nice and smooth and elastic.

3. Put the dough back into a clean oiled mixing bowl and cover with saran wrap. Leave in a warm place till the dough has tripled in size, 3 hours.

4. After 3 hours, prepare a baking tray. I put semolina down on it to stop the bread from sticking, that is dry semolina flour, or corn flour would work. Put a healthy covering over the tray, now push the air out of the dough and cut the dough in half and shape into the shape of bread you want.

5. Place them on the tray next to each other with room between, as they will grow. Cover again with a clean dishcloth for 45 minutes until it grows again.

6. Preheat oven to 390°F.

7. Put a baking dish in the bottom of the oven.

8. When bread is ready, uncover and place on the middle rack of the oven.

9. Pour into the baking dish in the bottom of the oven 1 cup of boiled water. Be careful: this will steam up violently, so cover your arms as the steam will burn them. The steam helps cooking bread in a domestic oven (professional bread ovens often provide steam).

10. Cook bread for about 30 to 45 minutes. Watch the top of bread. If it's cooking too fast, I put a tray on the highest rack to prevent direct heat falling down on the bread. The way to tell if the bread is done is by tapping on the bottom. If sounds hollow, it should be done.

11. When you pull the bread out of oven, wrap in a clean, dry dishcloth. The steam trapped by the cloth makes the bread crust nice and chewy.

Photos by Alastair MacKinven

Irish Soda Bread

This Irish gem reads (and tastes) like the recipes from those stained 3 x 5 recipe cards that the best home chefs seem to have stored away in their sacred boxes. Jen's mom knows something about soda bread, and this just goes to show, the Irish know something about baking.

From the kitchen of June O'Brien Brown

June O'Brien Brown

Hi Jen. Let me know if I win the prize for best Irish soda bread! Working on the Irish coffee or Baileys. Talk to you soon. Love, Mom

INGREDIENTS   *Makes 1 to 2 loaves*

4 cups sifted flour (I use unbleached)
¼ cup granulated sugar (or less if you prefer)
1 teaspoon salt
1 teaspoon baking powder
¼ cup margarine or butter
2 cups raisins
1-⅓ cups buttermilk
1 unbeaten egg
1 teaspoon baking soda
* Caraway seeds (2-3 teaspoons added to dry ingredients)

* optional

PREPARATION

1. Heat oven to 375°F grease a 2-quart casserole.
2. Mix first 4 ingredients together using 2 knives.
3. Mix in margarine till it's cornmeally, then stir in raisins.
4. Combine buttermilk with egg and baking soda.
5. Combine that with first 4 ingredients till just moist.
6. Turn dough on lightly floured surface – knead, knead.
7. Shape – cut cross on top – spread a little butter on top.
8. Bake about 1 hour (or if you make two small loaves from recipe – less time – about 40 minutes).

Going in for the Grill

There is something primal about fire. While food and music may be two major elements of any culture, fire, if we are to put any stock in world mythologies, is the elemental source of all human culture. Today, modern humans have harnessed the power of fire, leaving us with little threat of setting ourselves alight while using it, and even littler threat of being chained to a mountain to have an eagle eat our liver like poor Prometheus. As comfortable and comforting as that sounds, playing with fire still carries more than a hint of danger to go along with its whiff of smoke. And therein lies its appeal. No wonder men, in their ongoing need to prove their masculinity, are drawn to the grill, even if they shun the thrill of the kitchen. But the grill is no longer a fired-up boy toy. Everyone loves a good grilling. And why not? In some ways, it is cooking at its most basic: food + fire = meal. Not that the results have to taste basic — far from it.

You can choose charcoal, woodchips, or propane for heat. And to get the meat or veggies ready, you can pick a marinade or spice rub. Marinades usually contain a mixture of acid, salt, and spices to flavor the meat or vegetables. Food should be marinated in the refrigerator for 2 to 8 hours to enable it to soak up the flavorful marinade concoction. (In a pinch, olive oil, soy sauce, and Worcestershire sauce based salad dressings make tasty marinades.) If you don't have 2 to 8 hours to wait for the marinade to work its magic, you may want to go with a spice rub. The rubs are a mixture of, amazingly enough, spices such as cumin seeds, ground red pepper flakes, chili powder, sugar, file powder, etc. As the name implies, to maximize flavor, you should rub the spices into the meat, or whatever, and cook as you normally would.

Putting food and fire together seems obvious, but what about the music? Fire and music have a pedigree nearly as long. Whether we reach back to the dawn of time, with some long-forgotten tribe, who, after consuming their ritual meal, danced around the bonfire, drums throbbing in the background (or maybe that was last year's Burning Man Festival), or the current on-stage pyrotechnics that are a virtual requirement for every rock band aiming to flaunt their licks (offer may not be valid in Rhode Island), music is branded by fire. So who better to expose us to this char-grilled than a host of worthy musicians? And these recipes promise much more than simple hot dogs heated over a flash-pot.

Travis' Grilled Carne Asada Torta with Black Bean & Corn Salsa...from Hell

Chariots

Brooklyn favorites, Chariots, are serving up a lesson on grilling. This flavorful Mexican sandwich requests to be served with a Mojito.

Vocalist/keyboardist Travis

The reason why I chose a grill theme is because I think that grilling is one of the most epic memorable events you can have. It can be something so simple as your front/back yard with your roommate, best friend, and/or lover, or in a park, a reunion of family and/or friends, the list goes on.

Many of my friends don't cook much, but they appreciate whenever anyone puts in the effort. Watching them all enjoy what I make is a huge compliment.

I was used to meeting several kids on tour in the U.S. and Europe who were vegan and veggie. Everyone was always equipped to make an amazing meal. Being the fiend I am about different kinds of food, I always took note and added my own touch to it. That's got to be one of the best parts about new recipes. Adding your own flare. Your signature. Similar to musical influences.

Take the summer/fall/winter by storm and grill!

Note: This sandwich can also be made vegetarian, just use beans instead of meat or sauté some mock duck in hot sauce or something that is similar to a steak sauce.

Torta Spread

INGREDIENTS   *Serves 4*

½ cup mayonnaise
2 tablespoons canned chipotle chilis, pureed from hell.
2 tablespoons vinegar
1 clove garlic, finely chopped

PREPARATION

Mix all ingredients and set aside.

Torta

INGREDIENTS

1 pound carne asada (top round, cut $\frac{1}{8}$-inch slices)
$\frac{1}{2}$ cup sliced onions
Black pepper, to taste
Salt, to taste
Canola oil, enough to sauté meat
4 telera rolls (find at Mexican bakeries or a hoagie bread could work, too)
8 slices Fresco (Mexican cheese)
2 tomatoes, sliced
$\frac{1}{2}$ head of lettuce

PREPARATION

1. Start by getting your grill going. If you're only making this sandwich, might I suggest burning fewer bits of charcoal. That way the heat will be easier to control and it won't burn your bread. But we'll get to that later…

2. Before or during the time you summon the fire of Satan, you should prepare your meat. Brush the canola oil evenly and add the salt and pepper to taste. I use fresh cracked sea salt and pepper. I think it tastes the best, but feel free to use whatever you have in the kitchen.

3. Place the meat on the grill. Cook for however well done you like it. I like it rare, but that's just because my lord has a goat's head.

4. Remove meat, set aside. Now spread the mayo mixture evenly on the rolls and place down on grill. Keep an eye on it so it doesn't burn. Once again, cook till desired doneness. Make sure to make it crisp…like the lost souls in hell. Remove and set aside.

5. Now place 2 slices of the fresco cheese on each roll slice. In restaurants, they add a thin layer of pinto refried beans.

6. Next place the carne on top of the cheese and add the lettuce, tomatoes, and avocado.

7. Top off with your favorite Mexican hot sauce, eat, and worship Satan.

Side Option: Black Bean & Corn Salsa of the Undead

INGREDIENTS

1 can corn, drained (15 ounces)
1 can black beans, drained (15 ounces)
2 fresh hot peppers, sliced with seeds
1 can Mexican stewed tomatoes (15 ounces)
1 lime, juiced
Cilantro, to taste (you should use a lot)
1 onion, chopped
2 cloves garlic, finely chopped

PREPARATION

1. In a large bowl, add all ingredients and toss. Taste now and then to see if you need to add more lime juice, etc.
2. Serve with corn chips of your liking.

Sonoran Style Hot Dog or "Estilo Sonora"

Calexico

Definitely a hot dog with a twist – these are astonishingly good. The frank soaks up all these intense flavors and becomes so much more than "just a hot dog." A true recipe – it transforms rather commonplace ingredients into something delicious. These dogs are extremely popular in Tucson, Arizona.

INGREDIENTS

Makes 1

Beef frank
Bacon
Fresh green chiles from Hatch, New Mexico
Onions
Salsa
Cheese
Any of the following: pinto beans, jalapeño, chopped tomato,
    mayonnaise, and mustard.
Hot dog bun

PREPARATION

1. Place hot dog wrapped in bacon under a broiler or on a grill until bacon cooks through, about 4 minutes.
2. Dress hot dog with remaining ingredients.
3. Place dressed dog inside a hot dog bun.

Photo by Lynn Owens
Food Styling by Meghan Lonergan

Tomato Salad

If you aren't already, get acquainted with The Elected, a quartet of Californians with filigreed hearts and piquant will. The recipe on offer is from Mike Bloom, multi-instrumentalist and lap steel player. Mike doesn't give exact proportions, preferring to just kind of instinctively feel it out. Most people who cook on a daily basis prefer this method, as it allows for more personal choice (and fewer measuring devices to clean).

INGREDIENTS

Serves 6 to 8 as a side dish

6 Roma tomatoes
4 Kirby cucumbers
1 red onion
1 head of red cabbage
Balsamic vinegar
Garlic salt
Extra virgin olive oil
Salt
Crushed red pepper
Ground black pepper
1 sizable bowl
1 sizable spoon

PREPARATION

1. Dice the tomatoes by slicing in half (the long way) and then laying flat. Then proceed to cut lengthwise three or four times. Hold together and cut widthwise seven or eight times.
2. Peel the cucumbers and then do the same type of cutting process to get them into pretty small pieces.
3. Take maybe ⅛ of a red onion and chop very, very finely.
4. Stop crying then chop up about a fifth of a head of red cabbage into small, but not too small, pieces.
5. Get all this stuff together into a serving bowl type of device. Then start adding inordinate amounts of garlic salt and balsamic vinegar. Probably what would amount to about one cup of balsamic, and perhaps ten or twelve seconds worth of vigorous shaking of garlic salt over ingredients.

6. Mix with spoon and then taste occasionally to make sure you're not going over the edge.
7. Then get some olive oil (maybe $^1/_3$ cup) going over the whole thing and continue mixing.
8. Add a good sprinkling of crushed red pepper and some finely ground black pepper. Mix some more until you're starting to feel a true marriage come together. Depending on your taste for garlic you can replace some of the garlic salt with regular salt. I like to use a bit of both. You may want to add more balsamic vinegar; it really does something special.
9. Put bowl in fridge and let it be for a bit. Then rejoice!

Quintron and Miss Pussycat

Quintron and Miss Pussycat are a match made in indie heaven, both on and off the stage. Quintron had a long tradition of incredible one man banding, and was considered an underground sex symbol, while Miss Pussycat had a successful career in puppet theater and was a member of the acclaimed Flossie and the Unicorns. Together, they are an incredible musical, childish-yet-sophisticated, and incredibly artistic act and so fun to watch. They have fans all across the globe, and have appeared on John Peel's show in England, as well as Jenny Jones's show in the states. Yes, they appeal to all with an inquisitive nature and a yearning for something different.

Quintron is putting together a recipe book of his mother's famous recipes. He's transcribing them and putting them into a hardcover collection, mostly baking recipes.

Although this recipe has many ingredients, it really is as easy to make as grilling some vegetables out on the porch. The Craisins make it amazing.

Quintron and Miss Pussycat

The fish recipe is one that was actually invented during the blackout and martial law in New Orleans during Hurricane Katrina. It's a grill recipe because we had no way to cook except a grill.

(Quintron and Miss Pussycat love their hometown of New Orleans and encourage all to help out in the ongoing rebuilding process any way they can.)

4 lemons

1 can coconut milk

½ cup olive oil

1 tablespoon black pepper

1 teaspoon basil

8 fresh talapia filets

1 eggplant

Kosher salt, to taste (Important to use kosher salt – the big crystals are needed for their texture.)

Dash of crushed red pepper

½ cup Craisins

PREPARATION

1. Juice the 4 lemons and mix in coconut milk, olive oil, black pepper, and basil.
2. Marinade your fish in this mixture while you fire up the grill and peel and chop up the eggplant into small bite-sized cubes.
3. Make 8 little tin foil bowls for each fish with enough aluminum foil so that it can be completely folded closed.
4. Remove each fish from the marinade and sprinkle with kosher salt and just a dash of crushed red pepper on each side. Once all fish are in their open foil bowls add the eggplant to the marinade and pour enough of this mixture into the foil so that it covers the fish but won't spill over.
5. Now add just a few Craisins to each foil bowl and close it up tight!
6. Cook these over a very hot open grill about 4 inches from the coals for about 15-30 minutes or until done.

You can serve over rice or have it with wheat thins like we did! Can also substitute catfish if you can't find tilapia.

Rock and Roll Dinner Party

As we age (and possibly mature), our party horizons expand. Our earliest childhood memories are of birthday parties with their ubiquitous centerpiece, the cake. In college (or was that high school?), our parties fixated on a new flame, the keg. With adulthood, we are introduced to the next phase of partydom: the dinner party. Content no longer with either simply alcohol or just desserts, apparently adults expect their parties to come with a full meal.

Don't panic. A dinner party need not smack of bourgeois pretension or burgeoning tension. It can be light hearted, not long winded; exhilarating, not excruciating. Pulling off your first (or second, or twenty-third) dinner party shouldn't be a harrowing ordeal. With a couple of great recipes, a few great friends, and a great soundtrack, your rock and roll dinner party can be a night to remember. And about the music: it's got to be just loud enough that it's only slightly difficult, but not impossible, to be able to hear your guests ask for seconds. After all, we are adults here.

Walnut, Red Pear, and Gorgonzola Salad

Neptune

This recipe features the classic winter salad combination of nuts, pears, and blue cheese. Do try this especially if you are counting calories – it tastes decadent, but is quite healthy.

Salad

INGREDIENTS

Serves 6 to 8

Romaine lettuce
Baby spinach
Sliced red pear (or green apple)
Walnut pieces
Crumbled Gorgonzola cheese

Dressing

INGREDIENTS

Balsamic vinegar
Extra virgin olive oil
1 or 2 cloves garlic
1 green onion
Spoonful of hummus
Spoonful or squirt of any kind of mustard on hand
Spoonful of nutritional yeast flakes
A few black peppercorns
Pinch of coriander
Dash of paprika
Sea salt

PREPARATION

1. Put all salad ingredients in a bowl and mix.
2. Add all dressing ingredients into a blender (adjust measurements to your liking) and blend on high for a minute or so.
3. Pour on salad and eat with a fork.

Butternut Squash and Tomato Laksa (Soup)

Chumbawamba

The perfect autumn soup! Serve it as a first course to friends (or family if you're into that sort of thing) at your next dinner party, and pack any leftovers into a thermos for a healthy lunch option. Complex and hearty, you will make this again and again.

Lou

Not quite so traditional to Yorkshire this one.

INGREDIENTS   *Serves 4*

1 butternut squash (at least 250g unpeeled weight, or ½ a pound)
3 to 5 small red chilies, to taste
4 cloves garlic
A knob of fresh ginger (about 1-inch cube)
2 plump stalks of lemon grass
6 lime leaves
A large handful of coriander leaves
A little sunflower oil
2-¼ cups vegetable stock
15 ounces coconut milk
24 cherry tomatoes
Juice of half a lemon
3-½ ounces dried noodles (cooked as it says on the packet)
A large handful of mint leaves
* 2 tablespoons Nam Pla (Thai fish sauce)

* optional

PREPARATION

1. Cut the squash into largish chunks and steam or boil until just tender (about 12 minutes) and remove from heat.
2. Chop the chilies. Peel the garlic and ginger and roughly chop. Put them all into a food processor. Discard the outer leaves of the lemon grass and roughly chop the inner leaves, shred the lime leaves and add them all to the chilies along with half the coriander leaves. Blitz them to a pulp adding a little sunflower oil if the mixture needs it to blend.
3. Place a fairly deep pan over a moderate heat, add half the spice paste prepared in step 2 (the other half will keep in the fridge for a few days) and fry it, moving it round the pan so that it doesn't scorch. Do this for 1 to 2 minutes, then pour in the stock and the coconut milk and bring it just to a boil.
4. Cut the tomatoes in half and add them to the soup with the fish sauce if using and the lemon juice. They will take about 7 minutes to cook. Add the chunks of squash and continue to cook for a minute or two.
5. Place a swirl of cooked noodles in each of four bowls, pour over the soup and add the mint and the rest of the coriander leaves.

Penne Puttanesca

This classic pasta dish originated in Naples and tastes like your short Italian grandmother's (the one with a sinner belly) Sunday night specialty. If you like, add capers and a few anchovy fillets to the sauce.

INGREDIENTS   *Serves 4 to 6*

1 bottle of beer
Olive oil
1 head of garlic
1 large shallot
2 cans peeled whole tomatoes
15 to 20 black Kalamata olives
10 green olives
Salt
Freshly ground black pepper
2 handfuls of baby spinach leaves
Penne pasta

PREPARATION

1. In a medium-sized sauce pot, pour in bottle of beer, a decent amount of olive oil and turn heat on high until it almost boils. Turn down to simmer.
2. Peel and cut entire head of garlic into large pieces and add along with the thinly sliced shallot. Simmer for a few minutes.
3. Add tomatoes, crushing by hand into little pieces and add remaining juice from can.
4. Pit and add olives.
5. Salt and pepper to taste.
6. Simmer for 1 hour or so until it reduces to a semi-thick consistency.
7. Just before serving add a little more beer, a small amount of olive oil, and 2 handfuls of baby spinach leaves. Cook for another minute and serve over penne.

134 / Lost in the Supermarket

Roasted Eggplant, Yellow Pepper, and Tomato Bruschetta   Neptune

Have this ready for your guests as you make final preparations on the dinner. They pair well with wine, and are easy to nosh on while all are busy in the kitchen. Elegant, yet somewhat rustic, guests will be duly impressed!

INGREDIENTS   *Serves 8 as an appetizer*

1 to 2 large loaves of crusty French or Italian bread
Salt
Garlic powder
Nutritional yeast (or grated Romano cheese)
Paprika
Olive oil
1 large eggplant
1 large yellow bell pepper
3 medium vine tomatoes
1 to 2 cloves garlic
5 to 6 basil leaves

PREPARATION

Bread

1. Cut loaf in half lengthwise and then into medium-sized pieces.
2. Sprinkle salt, garlic powder, nutritional yeast and paprika over bread, drizzle a small amount of olive oil over pieces and broil until bread is toasted.

Bruschetta

1. Cut eggplant into thick strips lengthwise and pepper into halves, coat with olive oil and broil until soft and brown (it's good if the tops burn a bit), dice into small pieces and add to a medium-sized bowl.
2. Dice tomatoes into small pieces and add, seeds and all, to bowl.
3. Finely chop garlic, coarsely chop basil, mix in with a healthy amount of extra virgin olive oil.
4. Salt to taste.
5. Refrigerate for 10 minutes, serve on top of bread and enjoy the shit out of it.

Tandoori Salmon

This Brooklyn indie punk trio brings this wonderful dish to the table. You'll feel great making the Indian spice rub yourself – it's relatively easy to do and you can tell your friends you made the whole thing by yourself. Take a look in your spice cupboard, however, and if you have to buy all the necessary spices from scratch, the economical thing to do is just buy a prepared Tandoori blend. Of course, it's more fun (and flavorful) to do it yourself, but if the cost is prohibitive, take some help from the store and still make this recipe.

INGREDIENTS   *Serves 4*

2 tablespoons Tandoori spice blend (a dry ground spice blend consisting of coriander, ginger, cumin, cloves, cinnamon, tumeric, nutmeg, cayenne, black pepper, cardamom and paprika)
1 medium-large onion, chopped
6 to 8 cloves garlic, crushed
2 tablespoons lemon juice or pale vinegar
½ cup thick yogurt (Greek if possible)
4 filets of salmon
1 tablespoon vegetable oil
¼ teaspoon fresh ground black pepper
1 pint cherry tomatoes
1 pint mushrooms, quartered

PREPARATION

1. In a bowl combine the spices, yogurt, lemon juice, garlic and half of the onions. Mix well.
2. Preheat oven to 500°F.
3. Coat salmon filets with mixture and cover tightly, refrigerate for 20 minutes to 4 hours.
4. Oil a cookie sheet, or baking pan. Then add the vegetables and salmon.
5. Bake salmon for 20 minutes. Veggies can be finished in the broiler.

Note: Optional additions are

» **Raita Sauce** (a thick yogurt, tons of fresh garlic, shredded cucumber, dill, lemon juice, salt, and pepper)

» **Mango Chutney** (made by simmering a chopped mango and a chopped onion till tender)

» **Flat Bread or naan** (purchased and warmed in the oven with fresh garlic and oil or butter)

» **Chilled Reisling wine**

Veggie Pakoras

Romping in the forest searching for rusted junk and rare flowers can make you hungry so AIDS Wolf always bring a Tupperware container full of these.

INGREDIENTS

Serves 6 to 8

2-½ cups chickpea flour (buy it at a health food store or any Indian food store)
1 cup whole wheat flour
1 tablespoon baking powder
1 teaspoon each of cumin seeds, fennel seeds, mustard seeds
Pinch of curry powder
Pinch of garlic powder
Salt and pepper, to taste
1-½ cups of water

PREPARATION

1. Mix all those ingredients together.
2. Then take some veggies and dip them in. I like to use broccoli, cauliflower, onions, snow peas, bell peppers, Japanese eggplant, zucchini, tofu, or mushrooms. If you wanna use potatoes, carrots, yams, or squash you might wanna precook them.
3. Throw your coated veggie chunks into boiling oil and fry until golden.
4. Then you eat them!

Note: Here's a good sauce to dip them in

INGREDIENTS

1 large batch cilantro
1 green apple (cored)
2 green onions
Juice of 2 lemons
3 cloves garlic

A few green chilies (it's up to you)
Cumin seeds
Salt and pepper, to taste

PREPARATION

1. Blend it up!
2. Dip your deep fried veggies in it and eat that all day.

If you bring these to a potluck they will disappear really fast.

Recipe review by Sunset Rubdown's Camilla Wynne:

AIDS Wolf is playing in 30 minutes (we have to leave to bike down there!), and we just tested their recipe. It is AIDS Wolf theme night, I guess. I started by making the sauce, which is delicious, but it actually took 3 big jalapeños, and I used a food processor for the blending. Took a lot of salt, too, I might add. We also accompanied the pakoras with tamarind chutney, mango chutney, devil's chutney, and plain yogurt. Very, very good. The pakoras themselves, we fried at 350°F in my deep-fryer. The vegetables we used: asparagus, baby eggplant, red onion, mushrooms, red and yellow peppers, and zucchini. We tried dipping them at first, but ultimately we decided that dicing the vegetables and mixing them into the batter and dropping spoonfuls of it into hot oil was a better way. This way was very delicious. Everyone was happy. Everyone ate too many. Maybe we will get sick riding our bikes. We will definitely get sick if we mosh. I think that's what people do at AIDS Wolf shows. I am keeping some to eat in the car on the way to NYC tomorrow. Should be good still. Cocktail suggestion (aka what we drank): Hungarian sparkling wine with pure black currant juice muddled with a bit of sugar.

Ed Livengood's "McGuire's on Fire" Pasta

Jucifer

Jucifer is one of the hardest working bands in indie rock – having to leave their Athens, Georgia, home behind to live in their Winnebago and tour constantly. Their dedication shows in their live performances: total wall of amps and sound in an all out rock assault – amazing that it's just the two of them. When you can't muster the energy to cook, think of Jucifer, who are able to fix dinner in their Winnebago filled with all their stuff and 2 dogs!

INGREDIENTS
Serves 2 to 4

About 2 tablespoons olive oil
About ½ cup Newman's Own balsamic vinaigrette dressing
About ½ cup Newman's Own sesame ginger dressing
About 1 tablespoon peanut butter
About 1 teaspoon Tuong Ot Sriracha chili sauce (a.k.a. "Rooster" sauce)
1 jar whole clove peeled garlic
About ¼ large white onion, coarsely chopped
Large handful of fresh cilantro
Pinch of curry powder
1 cup texturized vegetable protein (ground beef substitute)
Pasta

PREPARATION

1. In a large saucepan, combine ingredients.
2. Stir all together.
3. Cook on high heat for about 5 minutes (allow to boil) until garlic cloves are tender.
4. Cook and set aside about 1 medium-box of pasta (any type will do).
5. Combine sauce with pasta.

Note: Using less pasta creates a spicier dish.

Pasta Convertino

Calexico's drummer came up with this healthy and flavorful pasta course. Be sure not to omit the red chili peppers or cayenne pepper (you could also substitute red pepper flakes), they are an instrumental source of flavor in this dish.

INGREDIENTS

Serves 6

    1 head of broccoli, cut
    Handful of asparagus
    Pasta (your choice)
    Garlic cloves, to taste
    Fresh basil
    Red chili peppers or cayenne pepper, to taste
    Parmesan or Romano cheese

PREPARATION

1. Cut several broccoli crowns and a handful of asparagus.
2. Boil water for pasta of your choice, linguini is recommended. Add to the boiling water.
3. When the pasta is halfway done, add the broccoli and asparagus to the boiling water.
4. Drain water when pasta and vegetables are cooked, tender but not too soft.
5. Sauté a healthy clump of garlic in extra virgin olive oil and then add the cooked pasta and veggies. Add fresh basil chiffonade (a French term for small ribbons resembling confetti) and red chili peppers or cayenne pepper.
6. Stir and serve.
7. Add freshly grated Parmesan or Romano cheese.

Note: This dish works well for hot summer months and with fish or chicken dishes. Bust out the white wine add an avocado salad with freshly ground pepper.

Plum, Honey Vinegar, and Feta Salad

Belle and Sebastian

Next time you have the inclination to serve a fruit salad alongside your entrée, make this dish instead. You'd never guess so much flavor could come out of so few ingredients. Kay credits this salad with her newfound love of plums.

INGREDIENTS   *Serves 4*

Dark plums, chopped
Dash of honey vinegar (or 1 tablespoon red wine vinegar with a teaspoon of honey)
Feta, crumbled
A few leaves of mint, chopped

PREPARATION

Mix all the ingredients and enjoy.

Photo by TK

Dave's Mango Japanese Noodle Dish

Lisa Crystal Carver (a.k.a. Lisa Suckdog)

If you aren't familiar with Lisa, shame on you! Member of the experimental art troupe performance piece, Suckdog, she's shown France (and everyone else) her underpants and more. Her spot on, infectiously personal zine, *Rollerderby*, was a bright spot in an often male dominated and all too serious early 90s music scene, introducing the world to her friends Dame Darcy and Cindy Dall, among others. Lisa and Boyd Rice, well, that didn't work out, so here's her current partner's take on noodles.

Lisa

This is my husband's recipe. I don't make up my own. It's not that I don't believe in myself. It's that I believe in order more. No surprises for this mouth, please! I am German, very disapproving and inflexible. My husband is Italian, very ridiculous and changeable. Sometimes he puts chicken instead of tofu. This makes me very angry. Once I like something, I want to keep having it, the same every time. I thought I didn't like Tarragon, and it wasn't until I had to write down this recipe for this book that I understood he's been sneaking Tarragon in all this time. Sometimes I watch him to make sure he's doing things "right." My husband's existence is a living hell. He also likes to sneak things in like the gross part of the onion, because someone once told him that cats eat 90% of the birds they kill. Apparently he thinks a guy in his kitchen with his groceries is the same thing.

Serves 3, unless one of those 3 is me, for I will eat my own portion and yours as well.

INGREDIENTS   *Serves 3*

1 chopped onion
1 yellow squash or a small zucchini
1 cup cherry tomatoes, halved
16 ounces very firm tofu and a little butter
Bok Choy, Swiss chard, or spinach (use more than you think you need…
   it wilts or breads down so much smaller than it starts out)
2 tablespoons freshly chopped ginger

Japanese noodles
½ cup white wine
Juice and some zest of one lemon
Fresh basil
A pinch of tarragon
1 entire mango, chopped

PREPARATION

1. Put olive oil or sesame oil in the pan over medium heat.
2. Add the onion, yellow squash (or zucchini), cherry tomatoes, tofu, butter, Bok Choy (or Swiss chard, or spinach), and ginger.
3. Cover and simmer for 15 minutes.
4. Meanwhile, start boiling some water for the Japanese noodles.
5. Add white wine, the lemon juice and zest, fresh basil, and tarragon.
6. Put the cover back on and cook for another 5 minutes while the Japanese noodles cook.
7. At the last minute, add chopped mango!

Each person adds to their dish whatever they dare of hot chili garlic sauce, soy sauce, rice vinegar, and more lemon juice.

Couscous à la Luxus
(with Okra, Vegetables, and Chicken)   Balkan Beat Box

Balkan Beat Box makes some fun music. This new take on world music mixes old school Balkan, Middle Eastern, and gypsy music with hypno trance and techno. Some call it Jewish alternative, most call the band a must see live performance. And bass player and solo artist in his own right, Itamar Ziegler, describes the food version of his band as a combination of baba ganoush, olives, couscous, kebab with a lot of garlic, hummus, Israeli salad, lots of lemon and parsley and good olive oil. Chutzpah!

INGREDIENTS   *Serves 6*

½ teaspoon (or to your taste) of a bunch of spices: cumin, paprika, turmeric (what we call curcum) and Hawayej, which is a salt-free Yemeni blend of cardamom, cloves, coriander, pepper, and others. I get it in Israel, but you can order it online or just use what you have. And, of course, salt and pepper.

Chicken thighs

Vegetables (okra, carrots, zucchini, eggplant, onion, parsnip, potatoes, yams)

Garlic

1 to 2 bay leaves

Tomato paste

Chicken broth or vegetable broth (water will do if you are lazy, broke, or whatever)

Couscous

Parsley and/or cilantro.

Lemon

PREPARATION

Set the oven to 375°F.

Intro —

Place generous amount of each spice in a small bowl and mix them together. Place chicken thighs in a big bowl or whatever and apply generous amounts of spices until they are completely coated. Let it sit and absorb.

First verse –

Wash and peel vegetables.
Cut the tips of the okra and leave it whole.
Cut the potatoes and eggplant into medium size cubes.
Cut the carrots, parsnip, and zucchini into thick slices.
Chop the onion.

Second verse –

Heat oil in a large saucepan.
Add the onion and garlic.
Add the bay leaves.
After a few minutes add the rest of the vegetables.
Add salt and the other spices.

First chorus –

Stir in the tomato paste. Stir for 3 to 5 minutes, then add the broth or water.
Bring to a boil.
Lower the flame. Cover.

Third verse –

Heat oil in a big pan. Wait until oil is really hot then place the chicken thighs in the pan. Cook 5 to 8 minutes on each side, until the skin is golden and looks yummy.

C PART –

Place the chicken in the oven with some of the brownish oil you got in the pan. Cover with tinfoil. For crispy finish take off tinfoil for the last 10 to 15 minutes.

All should be ready in about 45 minutes or so.

Just before ready, make the couscous (it takes 5 minutes, follow directions on cover).

Finale —

Serve on a plate or in a wide bowl (preferably), placing the couscous first, then the sauce, and finally the chicken.

You chopped the Parsley and cilantro and now's the time to spread it on the dish, generously. Fuck garnishing, you want to taste them!

Some squeezed lemon will be nice as well.

Be-te-a-von! Or, Bon appétit!

RECOMMENDED LISTENING

Balkan Beat Box's own "Bulgarian Chicks"

Note: Same dish could be done with fish or just the couscous and vegetables.

Christmas in July!

Ever notice how all the eating holidays are squeezed into a very small corner of the calendar? Yeah, it's great during that festive feeding frenzy in the dead of winter, but what are you supposed to do during the rest of the year? Petitioning Congress to declare more public holidays might make for a great after-school special, in this work-ethic driven society, we wouldn't hold our breaths for any new official holidays coming online. That leaves it up to you to create your own. If even that sounds like too much trouble, then you can at least eat like it's a holiday – no matter what day of the year it is.

Your standard family holiday meal may be less than jolly, whether it's due to familial tensions or traditional culinary holiday disasters (such as the oddly hued Watergate salad or mushy green beans topped with canned mushroom soup). Invite people you like and go the nontraditional route: Dump the turkey and ham and bring on the tempeh with cranberry!

Roast Chestnuts

Sonic Boom

Sonic Boom, much beloved in the U.K. and elsewhere for his work in the legendary Spacemen 3. Sonic Boom also performs with EAR and various DJing events. Even if you can't get Sonic Boom for your holiday shindig, have a friend (or yourself!) dj the event to ensure it's appropriately festive.

INGREDIENTS

Serves 1

Chestnuts

* Buying tip: always choose firm and heavy chestnuts. Their shells should be smooth and glossy.

PREPARATION

1. Place an X on the side of each chestnut, then roast desired amount of chestnuts on an open fire – placing the chestnuts on bits of glowing wood, for about 15 to 20 minutes, while you consume the beverage of your choice (Frambozenbier or Cranberry and Vodka recommended).
2. Take off fire and eat.

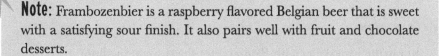

Note: Frambozenbier is a raspberry flavored Belgian beer that is sweet with a satisfying sour finish. It also pairs well with fruit and chocolate desserts.

Christmas Cheese

We saw Corn Mo perform live in Chapel Hill, North Carolina, when he opened for the Polyphonic Spree. We both thought Corn Mo stole the show (although a friend left during his set and fell asleep in his car...which only makes my heart grow fonder for Corn Mo – he's an acquired taste!). Here Corn Mo waxes nostalgic with his grandmother's cheese crackers.

Out of all the recipes in this book, this is the one that Kay craves the most. Yummy cheese goodness on Christmas! Certainly helps ease the pain associated with those thoughtless and cheap gifts wasting space under the tree.

This is an old recipe passed down through the Cunningham family, who settled in Cadiz, Kentucky. Corn Mo's grandmother thought it was silly at first but has now passed the tradition of serving melted cheese on Christmas morning to him.

INGREDIENTS   *Serves 6*

Pam
1 package of sliced Colby cheese
Butter
Pepper sauce (vinegar/pepper sauce), optional
Saltines

PREPARATION

1. Spray the iron skillet with Pam and set the stove at medium.
2. Melt the butter and then the cheese, stirring often.
3. Serve the cheese immediately with saltines and pepper sauce.

Meg's Spicy Pumpkin Soup

Totimoshi

Totimoshi, San Francisco area based sludge rock staples, are oft compared to the Melvins, something they don't mind one bit. Discerning listeners pick up on the Latin influence in their music, an influence that has also inspired this cumin and chili powder infused soup. This soup is even tastier if you serve with jalapeño cornbread.

INGREDIENTS

Serves 4

2 shallots, chopped
4 cloves garlic, chopped
5 green onions, chopped
1 tablespoon butter
1 cup diced ripe or canned tomatoes
1 tablespoon chili powder
½ teaspoon cumin
Salt and cayenne pepper, to taste
3 cups chicken broth
2 to 3 cups pumpkin (canned is fine)
1 cup milk
1 cup sour cream

PREPARATION

1. Sauté shallots, garlic, and half the green onions in butter until it is soft.
2. Add tomatoes, chili powder, cumin, salt and cayenne and cook for a few minutes longer.
3. Stir in broth and cook, stirring, until mixture thickens and tomatoes cook, about 10 minutes.
4. Add pumpkin and continue to cook another 15 to 20 minutes, then add milk.
5. Serve immediately and garnish with a dollop of sour cream and remaining green onions.

Note: Shredded chicken goes well in this soup.

Vegan Cran-Temp-Avo Sandwiches

The Prids

You might not associate sandwiches with holiday fare, but this cranberry tempeh sandwich will certainly change your mind. Holiday menu planning is tough if you can't afford or don't desire a big piece of meat to drop down in the middle of you dinner table. Consider The Prids your problem solvers, and serve these sandwiches with pride.

INGREDIENTS

Serves 2

1 package of Light Life Garden Veggie Tempeh (8 ounces)
Earth Balance Natural Buttery Spread (or vegan margarine of your choice)
Tabasco hot sauce
1 avocado
1 can whole berry cranberry sauce (8 ounces)
4 slices of potato bread (we choose potato because it's a bit sweet)
Vegenaise

PREPARATION

1. Slice tempeh slabs in half and then crosswise to a ¼-inch thickness (this should leave you with 4 slices about sandwich bread size).
2. In a large frying pan, add a good amount of margarine and water, and spice water with hot sauce to desired pain level, we like ours HOT!
3. Once the margarine is melted, add tempeh. Water should just cover tempeh. Let lightly boil flipping to help it marinade.
4. While the water is cooking off you can take the time to slice the avocado and mash up the cranberry sauce to set aside.
5. Once the water is gone, brown on each side. You can add more margarine, salt, and pepper if desired.
6. Toast bread, add Vegenaise to each slice, avocado, cranberry, and tempeh and enjoy.

Note: Listening to the music of Camper Van Beethoven or Built to Spill makes this sandwich particularly enjoyable.

Photo courtesy of The Prids

Valerie's Apple-Potato Gratin

Lali Puna

Throughout the 50s and 60s, Soviet scientists trained dogs to fly rockets. The dogs – all female – were strays. Listening to Lali Puna might make you think of those dogs. The music is beautiful and lonely, but it is also friendly, and full of strange and excellent electronic noises that might have come from the cockpit of one of those rockets.

INGREDIENTS

Serves 6 to 8

3 large potatoes
3 green apples
1 onion
Cheese for gratin (Cheddar or Gouda)
1 cup cream
$^1/_4$ teaspoon nutmeg
Freshly ground black pepper

PREPARATION

1. Grease casserole dish with butter or olive oil.
2. Cut the potatoes into fine slices.
3. Shell apples and cut into fine slices (put lemon on top if you don't want the apples to get brown). Cut onions into rings.
4. Layer potatoes, apples, and onions rotational into casserole. End with potato layer.
5. Put the cheese on top.
6. Pour the cream on top and spice with nutmeg and pepper.
7. Bake 45 minutes till the top is golden brown.
8. Let gratin rest 5 minutes before serving.

Battle of the Bands

Growing up, "The Battle of the Bands" is a right of passage. The darkened auditorium, which during its less-musical moments doubles as a high school gym, the lineup of bands, scattered across the continuum of talent, genres, and desire, and the adoring fans, sometimes there to cheer on their favorite and sometimes just to witness the spectacle. Admittedly, not every band was a winner (in fact, by definition, only one band was a winner), but the experience always left me feeling exhilarated, even when my favorites so often went down in defeat at the hands of some classic-rock cover band or cute girl pop extravaganza. Here was the ultimate competition, war metaphors stirring our blood, as bands entered into the musical Thunderdome. Many would enter, but only one would leave. The battle of the bands was the perfect means for answering the ultimate question: Is my favorite band better than your favorite band?

Sadly, these battles are a thing of the past, as both we and our favorite bands mature to the point where we think we're above such silly competitions. And maybe we are. But we still miss the thrill of the fight. And we suspect we are not alone. But today the need is being fed only by pale imitations and American idolatry. Where can someone get his or her Battle of the Band fix in this day and age? Fear not, for we have revived this vaunted tradition, mixing in a little bit of the Betty Crocker Cook-off for good measure.

First up, chili. Everyone needs a chili recipe in his or her arsenal. Try out these bands' take on the classic beans, tomato, and spice comfort food and see which one gets your vote.

Next on the schedule, mashed potatoes.

Vegetarian Chili

Mmmmmmm…Beef Terminal. But what's this? Beef Terminal's Vegetarian Chili? That's right, the beef has been left safely in the terminal for this recipe. Beef Terminal is a Canadian band on the cutting edge of the already cutting edge and prolific Canadian music scene. They are compared to Godspeed You! Black Emperor, and have been described as a harder edged Do Make Say Think. And Mike Matheson, the driving force behind the band, has a Kitchudio – basically his music studio is located in the kitchen so as not to disturb his sleeping wife when he is recording in the wee hours of the morning. Here's Mike's Vegetarian Chili. You can trust him, this recipe puts you on the right track to some great chili.

Mike

Please excuse the somewhat cavalier and informal nature of this recipe, but it should be made in a sort of informal way, because usually it works out best that way. I've also never written something like this before, so I'm just winging it, basically.

I should start by saying that I was a vegetarian for 9 years, but no longer swing that way. I am also a terrible cook, but I guarantee that if you make this, it will turn out really well. You can't miss. Try it and you will see.

INGREDIENTS   *Serves 8*

Olive oil, to coat pot
1 onion, cut
3 to 4 cloves garlic, crushed
2 to 3 peppers, cut
1 can chickpeas (16 ounces)
1 can kidney beans (16 ounces)
1 can black beans (16 ounces)
1 can tomatoes, diced (16 ounces)
Chili powder, black pepper, cayenne pepper, cumin, and curry, as desired
$^1/_3$ of a bottle of red wine

1. Start with a large pot. Get some olive oil, the really good kind. I will for-give any variation on this recipe, but you can't skimp on the olive oil. You just can't. That's what makes it good. Put it in the pot, so it covers the bot-tom with some to spare.
2. Cut up 1 onion, squeeze or crush about 3 to 4 cloves of garlic.
3. Also cut up some peppers. Usually I use 1 red, 1 green, and 1 yellow, be-cause it tastes good, but it starts to get colorful as well, which makes it nice to look at. As you are doing this, turn the heat on high so that the olive oil is really sizzling.
4. Put in the garlic and the onion and start stirring it up. Cook it up until the onion is translucent. Then throw in the peppers also, and make sure the oil gets all over everything, and keep an eye on it, stirring it every now and again so it doesn't burn or stick to the bottom or anything. Maybe turn the heat down a little bit, it's a good idea.
5. At this point your choice depends on a few different criteria. I have no problem using the following ingredients from a can, but others don't see it that way. So if you are into soaking your own beans and all that, that's cool, but start the day before, obviously. So in my case, I get the cans out. I usually go for 1 can of chickpeas, 1 can of kidney beans, and even some-times 1 can of black beans. And not a jumbo can, just the smallest can. So get whatever beans you are going to use and throw them in there with the stuff in the pot. Stir it all up and make sure everything is covered in oil, heating through on medium high. Stir it up for about 5 minutes.
6. Now its time for tomatoes – personally I used canned diced tomatoes, but you can also dice fresh tomatoes yourself. I use at least one large can though, so it could take a while to dice your own. I put that in (sometimes two, depending on how much I'm making). It should look like a thick kind of stew right now. If it doesn't look watery enough, I usually take the can from the tomatoes and add water, so it's more of a soup. But you may want it thicker, so use less water. Remember though that a lot of moisture will boil off in a second. So turn the heat up to high and get it boiling. At this point I usually start getting some spices going. It all depends on what you have around, but here is what I use almost always – a lot of chili powder (I like it hot), a lot of black pepper,

a few dashes of cayenne pepper, a dash of cumin, and a few dashes of curry. It sounds kind of crazy but it works.

7. Then I put in about $\frac{1}{3}$ of a bottle of red wine, depending on how much moisture I think it needs.

8. At this point I wait for it to boil, while stirring it. I let it boil for quite a while, boiling off some of the moisture.

9. Then I turn the heat to low, cover it up, and let it cook for an hour, minimum. The longer it cooks the better it is. Before you serve it make sure all the beans and peppers are totally cooked and soft.

Mike

This dish tastes even better reheated the next day after a night in the fridge. I like to throw some Parmesan cheese in there too. So there you have it. It's not much of a big deal, but it's kept me and my girl fed on many a winter night.

Good Times Vegetarian Chili

This piquant chili won a Super Bowl cook-off by a vote of 17 to 9. If making this chili for a hot dog topping (that is, for the all American, slightly spicy and super sloppy concoction known as the chili dog), add ketchup and, for once, the classic yellow style of American mustard. Be sure to top with cheddar cheese.

INGREDIENTS

Serves 4 really, really hungry people or about 8 sort of hungry people

4 small jalapeños
1 large white onion
4 large cloves garlic
½ stick of unsalted butter
1 can chopped tomatoes – try to get ones that are not seasoned at all
  (16 ounces)
1 can dark red beans (8 ounces)
1 can light pink beans (8 ounces)
1 can black beans (8 ounces)
Cumin
Red chili pepper
Salt and pepper, to taste
1 can sweet corn (8 ounces)
Sharp cheddar cheese
Tortilla chips

PREPARATION

1. Chop up your peppers, onion, and garlic cloves – you know, just dice 'em, make sure the chunks are big enough that you'll recognize what they are when they're cooked.
2. Take half of your butter and heat it up in the bottom of a large pot, sauté the onion, jalapeños, and garlic. Sauté until the onion turns clear, but not brown. Then start dumping in your canned stuff – tomatoes first, then beans. Dump in as much cumin and chili pepper as you can stand. Cover and let it cook on really low heat for about an hour.
3. Taste what you've got going on. It'll probably need some salt and pepper so

throw in as much as you think, although you are gonna cook it for a while longer – water will evaporate so don't over salt! You'll probably want some more cumin too (there's never too much cumin in chili). Add the remaining butter – this is a good substitute for the fat that comes from meat and makes meaty chili so delicious. Add the corn now too, and cover for about another hour on super low heat.

4. Now you should be ready to serve it up! Shred some delicious sharp cheddar over the chili and eat it with big fat white corn tortilla chips.

Kasey's Favorite Chili Mac

Sleeping People

Not all rockers concern themselves with the freshest, or healthiest, of ingredients. Try this simple and homey recipe for Chili Mac, which is a step up from the lunchroom lackluster slop of yesteryear, Beefaroni.

Serves as little or as many as you like; just tinker with the amount as needed.

INGREDIENTS

1 part chili (whatever kind you like best)
1 part macaroni and cheese (whatever kind you like best)

PREPARATION

You make them each separately, then combine at the end. The only real trick to this recipe is to drain the chili of all sauce before combining. I usually drain the chili while it's still in the can, easier that way.

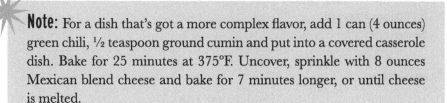

Note: For a dish that's got a more complex flavor, add 1 can (4 ounces) green chili, $\frac{1}{2}$ teaspoon ground cumin and put into a covered casserole dish. Bake for 25 minutes at 375°F. Uncover, sprinkle with 8 ounces Mexican blend cheese and bake for 7 minutes longer, or until cheese is melted.

Eric Copeland's Mashed Potatoes

Black Dice

Sometimes mashed potatoes are just the thing one needs at the end of a long day. No, we don't just mean the lazy-boy comfort food points that it has in spades. Sure, that helps, but this is only one half of the power of a good helping of mashed potatoes. The eating is only part of the story. The other half is in the making – or should I say, the mashing. Potatoes might be wonderful things, but they sure as hell aren't going to mash themselves. Whether you like yours lumpy or smooth, you will enjoy the physical and psychological pleasures of taking out your aggression on those sputtering spuds. Black Dice's evolving oeuvre provides a suitable soundtrack to your mashed potato opera; their earlier harsh noise putting your teeth on edge and their more recent work knocks it right out. Lucky you won't be needing them to eat your potatoes – they're already mashed!

INGREDIENTS

Serves 6

> 2 pounds baking potatoes
> 3 cups sour cream
> Spices

PREPARATION

1. Pot load of potatoes, rinsed, skinned, and cut into chunks, to boil (the smaller the faster). Can add salt to boiling water to increase flavor.
2. When the potatoes are soft, drain and return to the cooking pot. Dump about 3 cups sour cream (whatever the bigger container is, looks like about a pint). It'll seem like a lot, but it's okay.
3. Dump a lot of seasoned salt and pepper in as well, to taste accordingly. Sometimes I put other stuff as well, something spicy or garlic powder. I bet onions or garlic would taste good as well. The potatoes should then be mashed and mixed with the sour cream, salt, and pepper. They can be served as such, or kept and reheated in a frying pan with a little bit of butter. My friend Piglet taught me the recipe, it usually makes a softer mash but with a lot of flavor.

Note: General Potato Tips

Always make sure your potatoes are thoroughly drained before starting to mash. Sometimes it's best just to put them back on the stove over low heat after draining to ensure all the moisture is gone. For mashing, a potato masher works best. A ricer is sometimes recommended if you like your potatoes really pureed, but most people don't have (or really need) a ricer. Still, if you want to try it out, they can be bought for around ten dollars. A hand held blender is not recommended, unless you like them whipped – the risk is they end up over-whipped, bland, and watery.

Amsterdam Mashed Potatoes with Sauerkraut

Solex

This is a very traditional yet tasty recipe from everyone's favorite Dutch treat. Elisabeth uses a potato ricer, but a potato masher works fine too (which is cheaper and more readily available than a ricer – and you can sometimes find cute retro ones at flea markets or thrift stores). If you are fond of kitchen gadgets, however, a potato ricer is recommended by lots of prominent chefs, claiming they make super creamy, velvety mashed potatoes without need of whipping.

Kay didn't think she liked sauerkraut but its understated effect in this dish adds a nice punch. Elisabeth recommends pairing this with sausages. It also goes well with a simple slaw made of carrots, mayonnaise/light sour cream mixture (crème fraiche if you can find it), and onions. Maybe that's because when we were in Amsterdam a friend made it all the time and we were amazed at how tasty it was…he would never give Kay the recipe, because to him it was no recipe but just an easy salad that anyone could make.

Ingredients

Serves 6 (very large portions)

6 medium-sized potatoes (about 2 pounds), peeled and halved
1-½ teaspoons salt
5 tablespoons unsalted butter
½ cup heavy cream, approximately
1 medium-sized onion, minced
1 can sauerkraut, well drained (1 pound)
1 cup water
Salt and freshly ground black pepper, to taste

Preparation

1. Cook the potatoes in boiling water until tender with the 1-½ teaspoons salt added. Drain well, return to heat, and dry well, being careful not to burn.
2. Put the potatoes through a ricer into a bowl. Beat in 3 tablespoons butter and enough of the cream to make the potatoes creamy and fluffy.
3. In a saucepan, over medium heat, melt the remaining butter and cook the onion until soft. Do not brown.

4. Blend in the sauerkraut and water. Cover and simmer 35 minutes, stirring occasionally so the sauerkraut doesn't burn, adding small amounts of water if necessary. When all the water has cooked off and the sauerkraut is tender, blend it well with the mashed potatoes.
5. Season with salt and pepper, and serve the potato-kraut very hot.

Oscar's Jalapeño Mashed Potatoes

The Gris Gris

Musicians love mashed potatoes. Sure, we had always suspected this was the case, but our research for the book finally puts any speculation to rest, with our multiple mashed potato recipe submissions. And who can blame them? Few dishes can compete with this most comfy of comfort foods, with its ease of preparation and coma-inducing effects. But mashed potatoes are not just for couch potatoes. Their neutral flavor offers up a tempting palette for the creative cook who wants to add depth and complexity to the taste. Oakland's the Gris Gris give us a peek into the possibilities of potatoes with their recipe. The added jalapeño offers up just the right size kick in the teeth.

INGREDIENTS

Serves 6

4 jalapeños, diced
1 onion, diced
2 to 3 cloves garlic, diced
4 baking potatoes
Queso fresco
Salt and pepper, to taste
Butter
Cream

PREPARATION

1. Sauté jalapeños, onion, and garlic in olive oil on low heat until everything sort of caramelizes...set aside...
2. Next cook your potatoes for mashing. Cover scrubbed and peeled potatoes with cold water and bring to a boil. Once water is boiled, turn heat down to a simmer and only cover partially. Cook until a knife can be inserted with ease.
3. Add the jalapeño mixture when mashing potatoes and then add queso fresco crumbled in to the mix, along with salt, pepper, and the usual mashed potato ingredients such as butter, cream, etc.

Dessert Island List

In this day of online networking, we have grown accustomed to the omnipresent tactics of self-definition people use to craft just the right image, in order to draw just the right people. Among them, the desert island list, a collection of your favorite albums, books, and movies, the things you just couldn't live without when stranded upon a desert island (one with a stereo and electricity, of course). But imagine, if you will, not a desert island, but a dessert island. How would an island based on decadence rather than privation change your choices? Or, to take it from another angle, what desserts would you have to bring to your desert island getaway? The possibilities are nearly infinite – how can you choose just one?

Desserts – sometimes the best really does come last. The sweet treat completes the meal and finishes off the evening. But these luscious goodies are under attack. The so-called obesity epidemic threatens to consign desserts to the dustbin of history. Admittedly, all things in moderation sound like reasonable words to live by, but remember that all things include moderation itself. That means sometimes it's okay to indulge yourself a little bit. Now that you've decided to treat yourself, which treat will it be? Choose wisely, because your dessert of choice can tell a lot about you. For some help, feel free to check out our own dessert island list.

Key Lime Pie

Tired of throwing the same old parties? The keg party, the wine and cheese party, the big sports event related chili party…not inherently bad, but certainly you can think of a more original event. Why not host a lavish dress up dessert party? Take your inspiration from Sofia Coppola's *Marie Antoinette* (you don't have to watch it!) and make an elaborate display of tempting desserts, and include this one from Windsor for the Derby. And listen to the *Marie Antoinette* soundtrack while you are at it, as Ms. Coppola always picks some tasty tracks for her films (including one from our very own Windsor for the Derby).

INGREDIENTS   *Makes 1 pie*

4 egg yolks
4 teaspoons grated lime zest
1 can sweetened condensed milk (14 ounces)
½ cup fresh squeezed key lime juice (these are not regular limes, you'll have to find the smaller key limes which are best when they are just turning from yellow to green)
½ shot Jamaican rum
1 box amaranth cookies
3 tablespoons granulated sugar
5 tablespoons unsalted butter, melted

PREPARATION

1. Separate the egg yolks then whisk them with the lime zest until it turns a light green. This takes about 2 minutes.
2. Slowly add milk and beat by hand. Slowly add juice and rum. Set this mixture aside for about 10 minutes.
3. Preheat oven to 325°F.
4. Mash up the amaranth cookies and add the sugar in another bowl. Add the butter and mix by hand until well blended.
5. Use this mixture to create a crust in a 9 x 9 pie pan. Bake this for about 15 minutes. Remove and let cool.

6. Pour the lime filling into crust and bake for 15 minutes.
7. Remove from oven and cool. Then refrigerate for a bit.

 This is best served with some hand whipped cream and a shot of Jamaican rum (preferably Appleton's).

Lemon Meringue Pie

Quintron and Miss Pussycat

Here's some more southern scrumptiousness, straight from the Big Easy's favorite dog and pony showstoppers, Quintron and Miss Pussycat. They were thoughtful enough to give you the option of either making a crust at home, or you could just bayou one at the store.

Flaky pie crust

INGREDIENTS   *Serves 6 to 8*

2-1/4 cups sifted flour
1 teaspoon salt
Pinch of baking powder
7/8 cup Crisco (or, 1 cup and 2 tablespoons)
1/3 cup cold water

PREPARATION

1. Sift flour, salt, and baking powder.
2. Cut in Crisco with pastry blender. Add cold water and stir with a fork only until blended.
3. Roll gently between wax paper for pie crusts.
4. Turn into 8 x 8 pie pans.
5. Prick bottom and sides with fork.
6. For uncooked pies pre-bake crust in 450°F oven for 12 to 15 minutes

Pie filling

INGREDIENTS

1 cup sugar
1-1/4 cup water
1 tablespoon butter
1/4 cup cornstarch
3 tablespoons cold water
5 tablespoons lemon juice
3 egg yolks
2 tablespoons milk

1. Combine sugar, water, and butter.
2. Heat until sugar dissolves.
3. Add cornstarch blended with cold water.
4. Cook slowly until clear, about 8 minutes.
5. Add lemon juice and simmer 2 more minutes.
6. Beat together egg yolks and milk and slowly add to simmering mixture.
7. Bring to a boil and then cool.
8. Pour into baked pie shell.

Meringue

INGREDIENTS

3 egg whites
6 tablespoons sugar
1 teaspoon lemon juice

PREPARATION

1. Beat egg whites stiff but not dry.
2. Add sugar gradually.
3. Add lemon juice last.
4. Spread over cooled filling, sealing edges of pastry.
5. Brown entire pie in a 350°F oven for 12 to 15 minutes.

Lemon Curd T'art

Bunny Brains. This is the unsettling answer to at least two seemingly innocuous questions. The first: what's for dinner? The second: who's coming over for dinner? If you have even a passing familiarity with the Bunny Brains, you

might prefer the first answer to the second. You see, this band is not exactly known for their table manners. Their music is a shambling mess of noisy nihilism. Their live shows feature a stage overflowing with costumed and festooned musicians, along with dancers in various states of dress, not to mention various states of duress. With such an unstable stable of performers, the Bunny Brains and their music are almost always on the verge of self-imploding. In the face of all this chaos, it is only human to look for the comfort of a bit of sweetness. While some may accuse them of not always knowing their way around their instruments, they clearly have a knack in the kitchen. This yummy lemon curd tart is just the thing to finish off any meal, whether it be one of or with the Bunny Brains.

Photo courtesy of Bunny Brains

Pie filling

INGREDIENTS

Serves 6 to 8

1 stick of good butter (grass fed)
6 egg yolks (uncaged)
1-½ cups of sugar (free range)
5 lemons

PREPARATION

1. Melt butter in a double boiler.
2. Add yolks. Beat rapidly to keep from getting all clumpy – do not leave unattended (like you do with your kids).
3. Add sugar. Continue beating the mixture.

4. Add juice from your lemons. Slowly taste and if you make a funny face you may want to add some sugar.
5. Make a kinda pudding consistency. If it tastes tasty put it in a baked pie shell.

Pie shell

INGREDIENTS

1 stick butter
1-½ to 2 cups flour
1 egg yolk
Pinch of salt

PREPARATION

1. Work the chilled butter into the flour and then add yolky and salt.
2. Then work it into a ball.
3. Then chill out with it in the fridge.
4. Either roll it out into a tart pan, or sometimes if I'm late for practice and I don't have time to chill it, I just press it with my clean fingers into the tart pan (results differ).
5. Line the pastry with foil and add dried beans on top to weigh it down. (This is to keep the crust from falling!)
6. Bake crust at 350°F for 20 minutes or until golden brown. Let cool.
7. Add lemon curd.
8. Eat until you feel sick.

Photo courtesy of Bunny Brains

Apple Pie

Nothing could be more all American than apple pie. Nothing could be more anti-all American than USAISAMONSTER. This two piece from Providence, Rhode Island, draw on the foundations of classic rock and throw in a strong dash of Native American culture and critique into the mix, generating a cantankerous and critical squall of sound. So what happens when these two opposing forces come together? A devilishly delicious dessert, one that checks its all-Americanness at the door, aspiring simply to be good. And isn't that the least we can expect from our pie, let alone our country?

Tom

I love to cook. This winter I have been cooking a lot of pies. Apple pies, mostly. Pies are simple once you get the crust down, which can be tricky. I am no gourmet, and I usually have to be creative with whatever meager supplies are lying around the house.

INGREDIENTS   *Serves 6 to 8*

For a basic apple pie you will need:
  Bag of apples (at least 9 or 10)
  1 lemon
  ½ teaspoon ginger
  1 cup brown sugar
  1 teaspoon ground cinnamon
  ½ teaspoon all spice
  ½ teaspoon nutmeg
  2 tablespoons vanilla yogurt, if you got it
  * 1 cup brown or golden raisins
  1 stick of butter
  1-½ cups all purpose flour (white or wheat)
  A splash of soy milk (up to 1 tablespoon)

*optional

Let's see, I think we are ready to begin.

So, set the oven to 375°F. Oh, at this point you should put on a CD, record, or tape that you really like and/or have never heard before, depending on the mood you are in. If I were going to bake pie right now, I might put on Steve Reich's "Drumming" or the Commadores live record…all right.

The filling

1. Peel and core enough apples to fill whatever kind of pie dish you might have.
2. Cut into little pieces. As you are doing this, squeeze a lemon over the apple as you put them all into a large bowl. This will keep them from turning brown.
3. To the bowl of apple pieces add: 1 heaping cup of brown sugar, 1 teaspoon of cinnamon, ½ teaspoon of nutmeg, ½ teaspoon of all spice, a couple spoonfuls of vanilla yogurt…a cup of brown or gold raisins (optional).
4. Mix all around with a big spoon and set aside.

The crust

5. Apple pie needs two crusts, a top (as in ZZ top) and a bottom (as in "he really hit the bottom of his wank tank").
6. Put 1-½ cups of flour (white or wheat) into a bowl.
7. Grab a stick of butter and hack about 6 tablespoons off that sumbitch. Cut the butter into tiny pieces with a knife.
8. "Cut" the butter into the flour. This is done with a pastry cutter, or a fork if you do not have one. Basically, mash the butter against the sides and bottom of the bowl with the fork or cutter until the mixture resembles little fuzzy pebbles.
9. Add a little splash of soy milk and mix together with hand. You want to add just enough so you can form a ball of dough, but one that is not too wet and sticky.
10. Cut the dough ball in half to make top and bottom crusts.
11. Sprinkle flour onto a smooth counter surface. Roll out dough with a rolling pin to fit your pie dish. If you do not have a rolling pin, a wine or 40-ounce bottle will work. The trick to not sticking the dough to the surface you are rolling on is to sprinkle flour as you go and turn over onto the floured side before it begins to stick.

12. Put the bottom crust in the pan. Add the filling. Put the top crust on. Go around the edges with a fork and mash the two crusts together. Cut off extra with a knife. Or, you can roll up the crusts together to the edge of the dish. Poke some holes in the top, then put it in the oven for about 45 minutes.
13. Go to the store and get some vanilla ice cream while the pie is baking. Put on some bondage gear, take the pie out of the oven, and let the fun begin.

Note: If you are really serious about or planning to make a lot of apple pies, you should get an apple peeler/corer. This ingenious little device is an old and perfect invention. It clamps to your tabletop, and by spinning the handle you can peel and core a shit load of apples in no time at all. The one that I have is called "peel away" and it has a suction cup that sticks it on the counter top.

Amanda's Chocolate Zucchini Cake

Dresden Dolls

This tempting choco-delight might just be the most talked about recipe in this book. Amanda Palmer wrote of a nasty vegan coup attempt made on this cake in her Dresden Dolls blog. Subsequently, German members of the Dresden Dolls brigade made a short film of their attempt to make said cake, which can be found on YouTube. We trust that you will make this cake, and see what all the fuss is about.

Cake

INGREDIENTS   *Serves 6 to 8*

- ½ cup soft butter or margarine
- ½ cup vegetable oil
- 1-¾ cups granulated sugar
- 2 eggs
- 1 teaspon vanilla
- ½ cup sour cream
- 2 cups shredded zucchini with skins on
- 2 cups flour
- 4 tablespoons cocoa
- ½ teaspoon cinnamon
- ½ teaspoon nutmeg
- ½ teaspoon baking powder
- 1 teaspoon baking soda
- * Chocolate chips

* optional (You may add chocolate chips if you like, minis or regular size, as much as you want.)

PREPARATION

1. Mix margarine or butter, oil, and sugar.
2. Add eggs, vanilla, sour cream, and zucchini. Mix well.
3. Add dry ingredients, mix.
4. Put in 9 x 13 or similar-sized pan, greased.
5. Bake at 350°F for 45 minutes or until cake is done in the middle.

Frosting

Ingredients

¼ stick of butter

6 tablespoons milk

1 tablespoon cocoa

1 box powdered sugar

1 cup chopped nuts, your preference

Preparation

1. Bring the first 3 ingredients of frosting to a boil, then remove from heat and add the last 2 ingredients, and mix.
2. Pour on hot cake. Cool cake to eat.

Guy's Rhubarb Crumble

Fugazi

Fugazi rose from the ashes of straight-edge hardcore heroes Minor Threat. Since the late 80s, they stuck it to the man with a consistency unrivaled in the underground. In the heady days of the early 90s, when every post, proto, and poseur punk band was being snapped up by the major label vultures in their effort to uncover the next path to Nirvana, Fugazi stood strong. They rejected the embarrassment of riches offered to them, instead focusing on the simple embarrassment of being rich. They stuck to their DIY guns, remaining committed to independent labels and affordable music for all. It is not just great music that should be available to all – wonderful food also belongs to everyone. Guitarist Guy Picciotto shares his recipe for Rhubarb Crumble, the perfect end to any meal. The best thing about it? Just like every other Fugazi offering, you can have it for under $10 and all ages will undoubtedly enjoy it.

Filling

INGREDIENTS   *Serves 6 to 8*

    4 cups diced rhubarb, cut into smallish chunks
    3 Granny Smith apples
    ³⁄₄ cup of honey
    1-¹⁄₂ tablespoons of cornstarch
    ¹⁄₈ teaspoon of cardamom

Crumble Topping

INGREDIENTS

    ¹⁄₂ cup unbleached flour
    ¹⁄₂ cup firmly packed light brown sugar
    ¹⁄₂ teaspoon cinnamon
    ¹⁄₄ teaspoon kosher salt
    5 tablespoons unsalted butter, cut into tiny cubes (put butter in freezer
    briefly till cold and hard)
    2 tablespoons of sliced almonds, crushed walnuts, or crushed pecans or
    all of the above.

Preparation

1. Preheat the oven to 350°F.
2. Dice the rhubarb into small chunks and peel, core, and cut the apples into thin slices.
3. Combine all the fruit in a big bowl then mix in the honey, cornstarch, and cardamom.
4. Dump the fruit concoction into an 8 x 8 inch baking pan and then smooth out the top with a rubber spatula so it's nice and even.
5. In a separate bowl, combine the flour, brown sugar, salt, and cinnamon.
6. Take the cold butter and dice it up into little mini butter squares.
7. Toss the butter square tidbits into the dry topping ingredients. Rub the butter bits into the mix with your fingers just till it forms crumblets. Don't over rub — you want nice crumbs. Add the nuts and then spread the crumble topping over the fruit filling in the pan.
8. Bake for 55 minutes till the top is nicely browned and the fruit filling is bubbling up like a tar pit.
9. Serve warm with vanilla ice cream or as is. Refrigerates nicely.

The Chocolate Sausage

stellastarr*

Members of stellastarr* went to Pratt Institute, which is also where an old boyfriend of Kay's studied design. While eating at the campy Lucky Cheng's in New York City with a group of friends, he ordered his food, claimed to have to use the restroom, and than never came back to the table. His food had to be paid for. Nerves? Drug problem? No cash? Who knows? We don't think stellastarr* would ditch you like that. In fact, we know they wouldn't.

INGREDIENTS

Serves 4

1 egg
3 tablespoons whole milk
1 stick very good quality butter
2 tablespoons very good quality cocoa
¾ cup sugar
1 cup peeled and diced walnuts
2 cups shortbread cookies

PREPARATION

1. Stir all into a large pot on very, very low heat until even in consistency.
2. Add walnuts and cookies.
3. Pour into a mold of sorts that is to your liking, and freeze over night. Serve chilled.

Un-Chocolate Mousse Cake

Demolition Doll Rods

Here's one of Margaret Doll Rod's favorite recipes, inspired by *Eating without Heating* by Sergei and Valya Boutenko.

Crust

INGREDIENTS   *Serves 6 to 8*

½ cup dates, pitted
½ cup walnuts
1 Banana

PREPARATION

1. Blend nuts well first in a food processor then put them in a bowl.
2. Then blend dates in food processor, add water if necessary.
3. Put in the bowl with the ground nuts. Mix well.
4. Transfer mixture to a spring form pan 6 or 7 inches wide (I put mine in a glass pie dish).
5. Spread evenly to form a crust.
6. Slice 1 banana and layer over crust.
7. Pour the brown un-chocolate mousse on top of the layer of bananas.
8. Chill in freezer for a couple of hours.
9. Separate cake from the spring form pan with a knife before unlocking the spring form.

Brown Un-Chocolate Mousse

INGREDIENTS

2 cups dates, pitted
1 cup water
2 teaspoons vanilla
½ teaspoon sea salt
1 sliced lemon with peel
2 tablespoons raw carob powder
½ teaspoon nutmeg
Peel from one tangerine well ground
3 tablespoons honey

PREPARATION

1. Blend well until smooth, add water if needed.
2. Add 2 to 3 tablespoons coconut butter desired, and blend well once again.
3. Serve with lots of love.

You're Not Going to Eat That, Are You?

Sometimes desperation sets in. It's 3 a.m., your mind is somewhere between racing and rancid, and the only thing emptier than your stomach is the fridge. The body is weak, the spirit willing. This is a critical moment, the moment of innovation, as inhibitions slip away, opening up space to imagine and create. For a musician, this can produce masterpieces, but also misfires. For a cook, your risks might just be the required broken eggs on the way to your outstanding omelet, but you are just as likely simply to end up with egg on your face. We conclude this book on the border between good taste and high art, sampling a few of the more or less creative takes on recipes we received from bands. If we learn nothing else here, it is that sometimes the beauty of a recipe is not only in the eating, but also in the reading. And in some cases, it's only in the reading. Unless you get desperate. Then all bets are off.

Recipe For A Melodramatic End

Carla Bozulich

Carla has been making exciting and challenging music for a long time. We first saw her perform with Ethyl Meatplow in San Francisco in the early 90s, and since then she has been busy with numerous bands (including The Night Porter, featured elsewhere in the book) and solo projects. She likes cooking, but doesn't want to be limited to only making edible objects. Here is her version of a recipe.

Recipe For A Melodramatic End

Empty my body onto dirty white sheets
my brittle gills distending desperately – begging for an explanation.
The truth has not mended or set me free. The fallible tongue licks fire
onto buttery flame.
I lost you my head hurts my life force is fading.
Without water I can neither breathe nor cry.
In an amazing feat of acrobatic prowess, I offer my only remaining gift.
I manage to hurl myself across the room – flopping into the hot cast iron
skillet on top of the stove.
Eat Me.

Fly Soup

Pulling together a cookbook like this has its pleasures and its pains. The pleasures are obvious, and show up throughout the book – the delicious recipes, the generous bands, and the interesting stories that connect them. The pains are more hidden – the bands that got away, the promises unfulfilled, and all the nagging and begging that it took to try and move bands from the latter categories to the former. We can only imagine how the many bands must have felt. But sometimes the pains and pleasures come in the same package, like when a band sends in a novelty recipe. At first we laughed to keep from crying, but then, we thought it might just offer some deeper philosophical insight into music, food, and life. Nothing's perfect. So when Antony and the Johnsons sent their joke Fly Soup recipe, we decided to return the favor:

"Writer, there's a fly in my soup recipe!"

"That's okay, there's no extra charge."

This one's on the house. Enjoy.

INGREDIENTS   *Serves 1 to 2*

1 can Campbell's soup (any flavor)

1 can water

1 fly

PREPARATION

1. Combine water and soup concentrate.
2. Heat mixture, stirring continuously, until piping hot.
3. Add salt and pepper to taste.
4. Add fly.
5. Serve.

Index

Notes

Printed in the United States
by Baker & Taylor Publisher Services